The Bible and Kundalini Energy

THE NEW TESTAMENT

Deep Secrets of the New Testament Revealed

by Dorothy Elder

D1600003

This paperback edition published by

Doriel Publishing Company
Dorothy Elder
2557 South Dover, #75
Denver, Colorado 80227

ISBN 0-9631673-2-4
Copyright © 1997 by Dorothy Elder
All rights reserved

Library of Congress Number
97-65771

Cover Design: Thousand-petaled Lotus:
Symbol of Enlightenment
Spiral: Symbol of Serpent Energy, Kundalini

ACKNOWLEDGEMENTS

I am grateful first and foremost for the Holy Spirit which inspired this book. Second, my gratitude goes out to Corinne Heline and her writings on the Holy Bible which fed me many of my insights. Also to Charles Fillmore's METAPHYSICAL BIBLE INTERPRETATION for much of the symbolic interpretations. And then to those recorders, those teachers, those *rishis* who through the Ages have brought the World's Great Religions to us.

Permission to quote from the following sources is gratefully acknowledged:

Foundation for Conscious Evolution, Sonoma, CA, THE REVELATION, OUR CRISIS IS A BIRTH, by Barbara Marx Hubbard, 1993.

Doubleday, New York, NY, BREAKTHROUGH: MEISTER ECKHART'S CREATION SPIRITUALITY IN NEW TRANSLATION, Matthew Fox, 1980.

Bear & Company, Santa Fe, NM, ILLUMINATIONS OF HILDEGARD OF BINGEN, Matthew Fox, 1985.

Jeremy P. Tarcher, Inc., New York, NY, COMING HOME, Lex Hixon, 1989.

Bon Productions, Sierra Madre, CA, WHEELS OF LIGHT, A STUDY OF THE CHAKRAS, Rosalyn L. Bruyere, 1991.

THE BIBLE AND KUNDALINI ENERGY
THE NEW TESTAMENT

CONTENTS

I Corinthians 12:7-11

To each is given the manifestation of the Spirit for the common good. To one is given through the Spirit the utterance of wisdom, and to another the utterance of knowledge according to same Spirit, to another faith by the same Spirit, to another gifts of healing by the one Spirit, to another the working of miracles, to another prophecy, to another the ability to distinguish between spirits, to another various kinds of tongues, to another the interpretation of tongues. All of these are inspired by one and the same Spirit who apportions to each one individually as he wills.

PREFACE

Teaching on Kundalini Energy goes back thousands of years to Eastern religions. It is called by various names in other religions and the Hindu title for it is Kundalini. It is a spiritual Energy and I believe is basic to understanding the deeper teachings in the Old Testament as well as the New Testament. This word, Kundalini, may be unknown to the reader so I shall define it in simple terms. Later I shall go into more depth.

Kundalini, an Eastern religious term, Hindu specifically, is the spiritual Energy of Self-realization. It is called Shakti and is considered a feminine Energy. Serpent Energy, goddess, life force, pure consciousness are both Eastern and Western phrases designating this Divine Energy. Some interpret it to Christians as love, Beingness, Christ, Holy Spirit. It lies dormant at the base of the spine and is awakened through various methods which arouse the spiritual energy that can bring bliss, joy, creativity, and guidance for a spiritual Journey.

Now you may be asking, "How does that relate to our Bible?", "How does it relate to the New Testament teaching?" "Where does teaching on it fit into my understanding of Jesus Christ's teaching?" I am glad you have asked those questions. I hope to answer them in this writing.

My personal Journey has brought me to the realization of the experience of Bliss and creativity that is connected with my Kundalini energy. It is the love Energy of each one of us. We cannot continue to ignore it if we are to evolve spiritually.

I had started studying the Eastern religions and world religions in general as a part of my spiritual Journey before I wrote my first book, REVELATION FOR A NEW AGE, THE BOOK OF REVELATION. I was guided to bring the Eastern teaching into that book and the movement of the Kundalini for spiritual development became a core teaching. I continued to incorporate this teaching in the books that followed. Now, I have taken this teaching into a thorough interpretation of Biblical accounts because I believe that we of the West are awakening to the importance of it. Many religions are now openly teaching it to the masses, not just to the special group of Initiates, religious leaders, or followers of gurus. The teaching is also filtering into some Christian groups and is certainly becoming apparent in the holistic healing methods that are being practiced by many.

The Bible is filled with accounts which interpreters have taken literally on faith. That is fine for those who are satisfied with that interpretation. However, there are those who see much of the Bible as having deeper Truths which should be revealed now that humankind has discovered the power of the atom and the neutron. How this Energy can affect the human body, personality and spiritual choices are questions that need answering.

Understanding the Bible from a symbolic stance is not new. In the Third Century we have Origen, Greek writer, teacher, and church father, interpreting much of it from a symbolic understanding. Also Emanuel Swedenborg, in the Eighteenth Century, wrote many books on the Bible interpreting it symbolically or as he termed it as "correspondences" or inner meaning. It is said by researchers that Carl Jung, William Blake, Henry James, William James, Ralph Waldo Emerson, Thomas Troward, Bronson Alcott and many others were influenced by his writings.

As I have written eight books interpreting the Bible from the symbolic as well as literal position, many Seekers have been lifted up on their Spiritual Journey. I pray that the reading of this book will do the same for you.

A deeper interpretation of the Eastern teaching on the Kundalini Energy, called Holy Spirit by Christians, will follow. You will learn about the "miracles" as the result of Kundalini being active in a person or place. Some of the interpretations are based on a Christian foundation combined with the Eastern teaching. My Thesis is:

THIS DIVINE ENERGY, KUNDALINI, HOLY SPIRIT IS BASIC TO THE TEACHING IN OUR JUDEO/CHRISTIAN BIBLE AND TO OUR PERSONAL SPIRITUAL EVOLUTION.

I should like to point out that this is a teaching book. The reader may choose the Chapters that attract and read those. The same Thesis is repeated in each Chapter. The continuity of the teaching will not be interrupted.

INTRODUCTION

We are coming to a turning point in history—a new century. Each time this has occurred humanity has expected some great and wonderful explosion of new knowledge that will lift us up; or we will have a devastation of such proportion that none will survive or only a small percent who have followed the teaching of a specific religion presented by the prophets of doom.

This time is fast approaching. Each day, if you have your ear to the ground of these prophets, you will hear another theory. (The prophet says it is truth.) Each time we hear this we can become more depressed and say "What's the use. It is all predicted and will happen. I had just as well give up."

On the other side are the "Pollyannas" who predict only life and Light in our future. So where are we to turn?

Many have turned to the gurus of the East who have come to the West with their trunkful of guidance from the ages. This guidance has changed many from an outer focused person to an inner focused one as far as spiritual matters are concerned. That has made all the difference to that one, but somehow Eastern teaching does not always fit all the needs of the Western person, for our race consciousness is different. However, all of us, whether Eastern or Western, have within our consciousness commonalities called the collective unconscious by C.G. Jung, the great Swiss psychologist and religionist. These have not changed through the ages, but we have each interpreted them in terms of our own race consciousness.

Individuals have brought together Hinduism, Buddhism, Taoism and Christianity out of which has come the transcendentalist philosophy and the New Thought movement. This movement, started centuries ago, was slow moving because of the power of the Christian Church, but it continued to grow, for the spiritual understanding of humankind evolves just as our scientific and physical knowledge evolves.

There has been and still is much decrying by religious tradition-alists of this movement in consciousness. However, we are seeing now, little by little, a turning away of some adherents of the tradi-tional Christian teaching from that religion which is not in "sync" with known and accepted scientific, archeological, historical facts. The traditional interpretation of the Bible,the rock of the accepted Christian belief, just does not fit the facts and needs of the day.

Now this separating from the Church's dogma and creed has turned many away from taking seriously the teaching of the Bible. This is also true of those who are of Jewish descent who question the "old time" religion taught in the temple and synagogue. Thus we have a vacuum. Where do we turn—no priest, no preacher, no church, no cathedral, no Bible, no teacher, no rabbi? Where do we turn, for turn we must? Most humans in the West have looked outward for guid-ance for a fulfilled life; now the outer authority has declined.

The psychologist, the therapist, the writers, the seminar leaders, the multitudinous workshops have offered much help. The chan-nelers, the psychics, the astrologers have brought additional help but have not always fulfilled that longing for something else. What is that something else? Why are we not satisfied with all this mental re-search and teaching to help us overcome our unhappiness?

We have the physical culture gurus who try to answer this ques-tion. They say that to give all our attention to the development of our physical body with correct diet, massage, exercise, rolfing, reiki, acupuncture, drugs, herbs and Chinese medicine will be our answer. Happiness will be achieved; but that is just one part of our life.

Others believe and teach that yoga, in its various forms, medita-tion, contemplation, etc., will bring this balance. The trouble is that in Western culture people often do not connect these activities with spiritual growth. The teachers often do not understand what all of these activities are doing to the spiritual side of the individ-ual's personality and body. They do not understand the Divine En-ergy that is being aroused with these methods and so the results may be negative, indeed dangerous in some cases.

Through all these measures to help others have a super-ecstatic life, the sincerity of the teachers cannot be doubted; but sincerity is often not enough. Belief and sincerity have brought many to the brink of disaster because they are based on a fallible foundation.

All of these healers of the emotions, the physical and the mental are important, but the spiritual must be addressed also. Because many former members of churches have refused to follow the teaching of the Church, the baby has been thrown out with the bath water. I believe that rescuing this baby is necessary for our continued spiritual evolution. And what is this baby?

The baby that has been thrown out is the deep, esoteric, secret teachings of the Holy Bible both for Gentiles and Jews. The baby is the inner teaching of the Bible that needs a birthing in the consciousness of Western humanity. The baby, the esoteric wisdom, has the answer for many Seekers, but it has remained silent, for it was believed that humankind was not mature enough to receive it until now. It was too dangerous. To reveal these deep secrets would have made each person autonomous, which would have broken the power of the Church, of the family, of the government and of the society into which one was born. But the time is now for this secret to be revealed and I am guided with the help of many others to be one of the revealers of this mystery.

The question of where the soul goes at the end of this physical life has brought many philosophies forward. Many of these teachings have lifted the adherent to a higher level of joy and happiness as they tolerated this vale of tears until death would give them access to heaven. These teachings were sincerely given by those who purported to know the answers, and they have evolved many to a higher level.

Some of these teachings have put a weight of guilt and fear upon many and they have reached for alternative means to quiet the guilt and fear. These alternative means seldom worked but did give surcease from the pain of physical living for an instant or longer. Psychotherapy without consideration of the spiritual dimension of the personality, drugs, alcohol, devil worship, allegiance to cults— all have been tried.

Then there were few—very few—who stopped looking in the outer for the answers and turned within to their own spiritual guide. They were often aided by a vision of the Christ or a vision of Light, or an inner Voice directing them, or by what we call Grace. Then they started on their own individual Path to healing and were eventually guided to realize the secret of the ages. These few became mystics and wrote, spoke, served, started movements and demonstrated that they had found Truth for themselves. However, the followers were often not ready for this exalted teaching and it was "watered down" to fit their consciousness. They were stuck again and were prevented from experiencing the Ineffable on an individual Path.

Now we are coming to a period in our history of less dependence on tribe, family, social structure or authorities in government and Church and are becoming more individualistic. This provides us the freedom to follow our own inner Guide and break away from the status quo. This movement in the individual, of course, needs freedom from physical wants and needs. Emotional and intellectual needs are fulfilled when the spiritual needs are taken care of and vice versa. And so we are ready. Where do we turn then?

We turn within to the Guide. Our Inner Guide is honored. It is called by various names—our own personal one, or what our religion has taught us to call It. Whatever. We know It to be individual and special only for us.

It is this Inner Spirit that is our true identity. That is who we really are. Not an American, or German or African. Not a man or a woman. Not a democrat or republican. Not white, black, yellow, red or brown. Not any thing nor person, but this Inner Spirit.

This Spirit is called by many names. It has been a mystery for most. It has been spoken of by all religions under one guise or another. It has been described as an Energy, as a Voice, as a god, as a goddess, as the creator of all, as she, as he, as life, light, truth, joy, ecstasy, guide, Savior, father, mother, and ki, chi, kundalini, shakti, hygeia (Greek), consciousness, fire, and Holy Spirit, plus many, many others.

It has always carried a veil of mystery placed there by not only the religion's teaching but by those who have experienced It. This is because when we become conscious of It and activate It, we may suffer dire effects. We will go into that later.

This leads me to my Thesis of this book, which is that this Divine Energy, this Kundalini, this Holy Spirit is basic to the teaching in our Judeo/Christian Bible. This is such an important teaching among all religions—indeed maybe the central teaching—that I believe it is taught in our own Bible through symbology. So I am going to uncover some of those teachings in an effort to lead us to the realization that the effects of the movement of this Divine Energy is what each of us has been searching for to bring us the Ecstasy we know awaits us. This Divine Energy is feminine. It is Wisdom, Sophia, Mary, the Christ.

There are those, especially Bible scholars, who may say that I am going into the psychic realm which they decry but I have been given this Commission and I have no choice but to carry it out. For some it will not be Truth—for others it will answer many questions that have plagued them on their spiritual Journey.

Sometimes I shall depend on references to the writings of other authors who have studied the symbolic meaning of accounts in the Bible and support my Thesis. I shall also be guided by that inner well of secret knowledge which lies dormant in my unconscious, in my Self, in that Spirit of Christ, that has taught me and accompanied me through this lifetime and many others.

The Old Testament accounts of the awakening of this Divine Energy has also been kept secret from those of us who were not privileged to be Initiates, Kabbalahists, disciples of various religious teachings. These who were so honored became mystics and were often given great honor but sometimes extreme religious censure. Mysticism is now exploding as more and more are prepared to find that Inner Knowing and let that Energy be the Guide and focus of life. Many of us are now reaching that stage of our spiritual Journey. The teachings of the Bible can inform and prepare us for this spiritual baptism. This teaching on the Kundalini as it relates to our Bible and especially to the New Testament, may do just that for you.

Just to whet your appetite, let us look at the myth of Moses and the burning bush (See Exodus 3). I use the word myth advisedly for it is from myth that we gain much secret knowledge albeit couched in symbolic terms. A myth is not an untruth but demonstrates deep truth and has been the basis of many religions. To take a very small slice of Moses' story let us start with his forty years in the desert before he received his commission. His wife was named Zipporah (little bird) and his son, Gershom (exile). Married to little bird symbolizes married to flighty thoughts some of which soar high above the mundane world. From this came forth a sense of exile, for when Moses (drawing forth) had thoughts above the intellect or world then something else is drawn forth and a feeling of being exiled is born.

Moses had a Purpose to fulfill as we all do. One day he had his Light experience, a rebirth, a total change, and his Purpose was revealed to him. On a mountain (high state of consciousness) he "saw" a burning bush which was not destroyed by the fire. So what was this seeming fire? Let us suggest that his Divine Energy, his chi, his Holy Spirit was very, very active in his body and consciousness. This Holy Spirit filled his spine with Light along with the nerve centers and chakras. (Remember the bush was not destroyed.) His

Purpose came to him because of his En-light-ened condition. His intellect, his reasoning power, was given over to his Intuition and he had a conversation with his Inner Knowing and "heard," followed, and had a life-changing experience. Where he stood was Holy Ground and he was told to remove his shoes, or remove anything from his understanding, his feet.

If you have studied or read any books on the experiences of many men and women who have had the Light and Voice experience, you will recognize this as a viable explanation. (Richard Bucke describes many like experiences in his book, COSMIC CONSCIOUS-NESS.) How it happens is the secret that is being revealed now as mystics and researchers uncover that which the Eastern religions, the esoteric religions, have known through the ages.

Well, if you feel lost already, please hang in there or here, for I will simplify this in the following pages. (At least I hope it will be simplified.) An explanation of the movement of the Kundalini through the spine, chakras and nerves follows in the ADDENDUM.

As I have mentioned, I have studied this secret of the Kundalini for many years and have written about it in many of my books. The main reason I became interested was because of my own experiences as this Divine Energy awakened in me while I was having dream analysis with a Jungian analyst who understood it and its movement. These "out of this world" experiences came to me without conscious effort on my part, but I am not alone. There are those in the West who are testifying to these experiences also, and are not connected with any organized religion, or they may be. Many of the leaders in the traditional religions would consider this idea pure insanity, but when we have authors such as Gopi Krishna of India and Richard Bucke, a Westerner, who wrote and spoke on this subject eloquently and from their own experience and study, it is time to awaken. Teresa of Avila and other saints have written about their experiences with it. Also, the Siddha Yoga movement is strong in the United States. Muktananda, the guru of this movement, awoke this Fire in the body and consciousness of many who are lifting the consciousness of the world. Gurumayi followed him as the Guru of that Order. According to an article in their magazine, DARSHAN, Vol. 41, 42 of 1990, all religions or spiritual traditions speak of Kundalini this inner spiritual power, in one form or another. Mystery religions of ancient Egypt, Greece, Rome, Gnosticism, Cabalistic and various secret brotherhoods, are mentioned in the literature.

It is well documented that Initiates of the Rosicrucians, Alchemists, Freemasons also had secret teachings on this Divine Energy.

One of my major themes will be the need to balance the masculine and feminine Energies in our consciousness as well as in our body and affairs. So much of our Judeo/Christian religion has been based on the patriarchal concept of God that the feminine has often been lost sight of. We are evolving to the concept of God as Unity. The feminine must be balanced with the masculine if we are to achieve Unity or Oneness. Until one accepts the androgyny of God, he/she cannot reach that Oneness.

The Kundalini is feminine and the same as the Holy Spirit which has been covered up by the concept of God the Father. This will be a major jump for the Jew and Christian, but I think the time is here when we must let go of the concept of God being either gender, and realize that we as humans have made God in our own image. The Godhead, that Universal Energy, would better be alluded to as It.

Other religions than Judaism and Christianity have seen this Transcendent Energy we have entitled God the Father, as Mother, Father/Mother, as Friend, as Brother, as Sister, etc. I should like to quote some of these found in the book, WORLD SCRIPTURE, page 95, by International Religious Foundation:

> The Valley Spirit never dies.
> It is named the Mysterious Female.
> And the Doorway of the Mysterious Female
> Is the base from which Heaven and earth sprang.
> It is there within us all the while;
> Draw upon it as you will, it never runs dry.
>
> Taoism, Tao Te Ching 6

From Hinduism: I am Father and Mother of the world.
>
> Bhagavad Gita 9.17

From Sikhism: Thou art Father, Mother, Friend, Brother. With Thee as succorer in all places, what fear have I?
>
> Adi Granth, Majh M.5,

From Shinto: All ye under the heaven! Regard heaven as your father, earth as your mother, and all things as your brothers and sisters.
>
> Oracle of Atsuta

From Confucianism: Heaven and Earth are the father and mother of the ten thousand things.

Book of History 5.1.1.
The Great Declaration

From Native American: Mother Earth have pity on us and give us food to eat!
Father, the Sun, bless all our children and may our paths be straight!

Blackfoot Prayer

There are, of course, many other religions with this same concept. I shall not go into the goddess worship of religions of the past except as it applies to my interpretation of the Bible passages. There are many books written on this subject, one of which is WHEN GOD WAS A WOMAN by Merlin Stone.

The Church, the Catholic Church, we know deleted much from the original text of the Holy Bible. We now have the Nag Hammadi Scrolls and the Dead Sea Scrolls which are slowly but surely coming to light. Both of these may reveal some of this scripture which has been deleted; but no matter, for we will work with what we have and uncover this deep secret which will awaken many to the Truth of their Being and verify their own experience.

The ADDENDUM will deal with a discussion of this Divine Energy and its activation from other religions of the world. We shall work our way through the New Testament. It will be necessary for you to set aside your reasoning, logical, masculine intellect at times and soar with the feminine half of your brain. Let your feeling nature respond to what is written and thus give your Spirit a chance to speak. Part of this book will be written from the left brain, masculine level, but when the writing is inspired by the Spirit, my Intuition, you will recognize it. Then let your right brain reign. It will be a wondrous Journey for you, based on the secrets that have been hidden for ages.

My references will be noted as we go along. I may quote from authors you have not heard of because their writing is so "way out" that the conventional has by-passed it. So let us have an exciting journey together. I shall be learning as I write and hope enlightenment will begin to function in love as you accept your own Inner Light and Voice experience.

The following Bibles have been used:
  Revised Standard Version - RSV
  New Revised Standard Version - NRSV
  New International Version - NIV
  The Jerusalem Bible - JBV
  King James Version - KJV
  Good News Version - GNV
The Revised Standard Version has been used unless otherwise noted.

Chapter I

INSPRIRATIONS FROM THE CHRIST

The New Testament of the Judeo/Christian Bible has affected the lives, the hopes, the souls, the destiny of millions of people throughout nearly 2000 years since the advent of Jesus. The Wisdom portrayed in it has the feminine quality of the Kundalini, the Holy Spirit, the Holy Ghost (KJV). Its interpretation has comforted, cajoled, guided, defeated human beings and still does. It is a mystery in many ways and yet it is perfectly clear to those who believe.

As I have stated my interpretation will be more symbolic than literal, although I do accept much of the accounts as true representations of Jesus Christ's teaching. My purpose is not to discount the teachings but to enhance them by an esoteric interpretation for a deeper meaning.

The Kundalini is referred to as the Comforter, the Spirit of Truth, the Counselor. The Holy Spirit fits our Thesis on which this book is written. It is that Holy Energy that gives life to all, heals, guides and can be used or can use us for a higher, deeper work than we have ever envisioned.

Much of the teaching in the Book of John supports my Thesis, as do other Books, but in the interest of brevity I shall concentrate my interpretation on the Book of John. It is the most mystical tome and recounts the deepest teachings of Jesus the Christ. It is in this book that Jesus promised that he would send the Holy Spirit to his disciples.

We shall discuss the ministry of Jesus, his healings and his teaching his disciples how to arrouse this Energy as they healed. We shall discuss his transfiguration and his message to each of us personally. Later we shall discuss Paul and some of the disciples who carried on

1

the admonition of Jesus to "go ye into all the world preaching the gospel."

According to the latest scholarly research it is believed the dates of the various Gospels are as follows:

Matthew, written by Matthew the Disciple in A.D. 70
Mark, written by John Mark, A.D. 65
Luke, written by Luke the Beloved Physician, after A.D. 70
John, written by John the Disciple, A.D. 85 or later

The Book of Acts was also written by Luke after A.D. 70. The writings of Paul, 13 books, were written before Acts, the time ranging from A.D. 51-66. The Book of Revelation was written by John (whether the Disciple is not agreed upon) in approximately A.D. 95.

As we advance into the ministry of Jesus, I should like to discuss the authenticity of the events and teachings of Jesus Christ which were recorded by the various Gospel writers. Many question whether the "miracles" performed by Jesus really happened. This is a question that will need answering by each individual.

It is accepted that the Gospels were written about 35 to 65 years after the so-called death of Jesus. We do not know that these authors were well educated, with the possible exception of Luke. The accounts of the teachings and actions of Jesus do not always bear consistency from one writer to another although they may record the same incident. How they could be as consistent as they are, should be our major question. I should like to suggest the following:

I believe that the Christ, either in the Light body of Jesus or by inspiration, was near to the founders of the Christian Church, as well as to the writers of the Gospels. He had said to his disciples in John 14:18, "I will not leave you desolate, I will come to you." This was spoken just before his crucifixion. I believe that he came to the writers of the Gospels and inspired them to write these accounts. These were inspired men and as they opened their intuitive faculty to the Inner Voice, the Christ of Jesus spoke through them and they recorded the fine details of his life and teachings.

But some may ask, "Why are there differences in the reporting of the same incident?" My reply is that the Intuitive Voice comes to each of us with the same Truth, but due to our conditioning, our life experiences, our reluctance to express what we "hear," and the level of our consciousness, we record what we "hear." That level can distort some of what comes from our Intuition.

Intuitive Guidance needs translating into words or artistic endeavor, or scientific breakthrough. If we are to record it perfectly we must be free of any influence from our human conditioning. These men were not free of the desire to speak to certain segments to which they were loyal. John Shelby Spong in RESCUING THE BIBLE FROM FUNDAMENTALISM says that Matthew wrote his Gospel relating it more to Jewish ideas. John Mark, whose Gospel was written first and who had not been Jesus' personal follower, wrote for the community of Christians in Rome. Luke, the physician, wrote for the Gentile Christians. John, the least literal and least objective, had great dependence on the Hebrew Scriptures, on Proverbs and the Apocryphal books of Sirach, Wisdom of Solomon, Baruch and the Book of Enoch. The Book of John is based on the Wisdom tradition. John's Gospel is the most mystical of all.

Thus, each of these authors were affected by their past or their present need to address a certain group of people. They each "heard" from the level of their ability to put into words that which would affect their listeners. This does not make them any less authentic. It only proves what Jesus taught, that we must go within, listen to our own Inner Christ, the Inner Voice, and speak and act from There. Each author was Guided by that Inner Christ and recorded the best they could. The intellect can be fallible when we are recording from our Inner Truth.

I believe that the Christ came to them and inspired them. They perhaps did not see him in his Light Body, but perhaps they did. He gave them details of his life and service to his Father. There are accounts of Jesus' experiences where it appeared no one was with Jesus, i.e., the Garden of Gethsemane and the wilderness experience of temptations. If we take these accounts literally there were no witnesses mentioned. However, when we read these accounts from the esoteric level, we do not need to be told of a witness. In any case we know that the Christ is still with us, and I believe gives those who are interested guidance for interpreting the scripture and guidance for their Journey to fulfill their Purpose. This Christ is not Christian, Muslim, Jew or Hindu. This Christ is One in each and all. This Christ is the Holy Spirit and this explains why there is so much similarity in different religious teachings. This Christ is that Universal Presence which has motivated humankind to a higher level of Love and Truth. "I am the way, the truth, and the life." (John 14:6) I AM is that Presence within and all around us.

3

The Gnostics also taught that the Christ, in the Light Body, appeared to many of his followers and opened to them, through visions and divine insights, the divine mysteries. (See the NAG HAMMADI LIBRARY, James M. Robinson, Editor.)

With this background, let us now proceed to a discussion of the Annunciation of Jesus' advent into the world, his baptism, his message to us, his healings and teachings through his parables and his Transfiguration. We shall also cover, briefly, the Book of Acts and the Book of Revelation. The teachings are for each of us, and I shall demonstrate how the Divine Energy, the Kundalini, was active in each of the incidents I have chosen to discuss.

Chapter II

THE ANNUNCIATION

In opening this section on the New Testament it is imperative that I discuss the birth of Jesus through the Virgin Mary. This Mary, the greatest Christian Mystic, has inspired and led the feminine aspect of the Catholic Church for thousands of years. Her perfection has been presented for 2000 years to the Western World of Catholicism and Protestantism. She is said to have had her Assumption, body and soul, into Heaven, which is beyond our human perception or understanding. This feminine aspect of humanity has taken its place in the liturgy and theocracy of the Catholic Church, but not so much in the Protestant teaching. She seems to be worshipped in the predominantly Catholic countries more than her son Jesus. It is the statue of Mary, the Virgin, that is often standing before the cross of her son Jesus. Jesus is usually depicted hanging on the cross while Mary is in the form of a statue standing firmly on *terra firma*. The feminine aspect of the Spirit is thus honored.

However, I shall present a more symbolic interpretation of Mary, of the Holy Spirit, and Jesus, Mary's son. All of this will come from the deepest aspect of my Knowing and far supersedes any interpretation from my intellect that I could present.

This interpretation does not reduce the interpretation that the Church has given, but for those who are ready it will enhance that teaching.

(I am writing this to the strains of "Amazing Grace" at the International Catholic Youth Day Conference in Denver, Colorado, in 1993. It is Grace that has brought me to this place in my Eternal Journey. As I listened to Pope John II present his Homily at the Mass, I was recording a verse from Mary's Magnificat, and I heard him reading the same verse concurrently. This synchronistic happening came from the Spirit which is One with each of us.)

In nearly all the religions of the world we find a trace of a divine woman being the mother of an incarnate Deity. The goddess mother and child is pictured in many temples and ancient worship centers.

The Annunciation of the Birth of Jesus is taken from Luke 1:26–38. Let us quote several of these verses.

> The angel said to her, "Do not be afraid, Mary, for you have found favor with God. And now, you will conceive in your womb and bear a son, and you will name him Jesus." (Verses 30, 31, NRSV)

> The angel said to her, "The Holy Spirit will come upon you, and the power of the Most High will overshadow you, therefore the child to be born will be holy; he will be called Son of God." (Verse 35 NRSV)

Here we have Mary having that Mystical experience of seeing a Light Being and "hearing" a heavenly message. We are all potential Mystics. A like experience may come to each of us sometime on our Journey.

An angel, Gabriel, sent from God, came to Galilee, which symbolizes energy of life, soul energy, power force. Nazareth, the town where Mary lived, symbolizes a branch, a shining. Gabriel symbolizes realization and demonstration of the I AM.

Divine Realization came to Mary, who symbolizes the divine motherhood of love. She received it through intuition. We give birth to the great realization of our Spirit through our intuition. Out of the coming together of intuition, and the demonstration of the Holy Spirit, comes our realization of the holiest, the Christ, the Son, the Daughter, the I AM.

Annunciation comes to each of us from God, the Universal Presence, and touches our feminine soul, and the realization of the Holy Spirit, the Christ, is born in our consciousness. This is the Second Coming of the Christ. It is for Everlasting and comes to all human beings in one way or another. For Mary, the virgin, it came from an Angel and a Voice.

We are all virgin. Our soul is virgin. The Spirit within that soul needs birthing into our Realization and our Journey begins back to the Kingdom of Heaven. Our Ascension begins. It requires more than a physical connection to the Church, the minister, the Pope.

It must be an Inner Birth from the womb of our soul. From there the Spirit is recognized and the Glory of the Lord, the Angels, will sing Glory, Glory, Glory within and around us.

We may try to deny this miracle from our human intellect, but it will not be denied. It will be born for and from the Glory of the Universal Presence.

We may protest when this Gift comes upon us. We may say with Mary, "How can this be, since I am a virgin?" (Verse 34)

What does being virgin mean? We are all virgin in our spiritual Journey until we realize the feminine aspect of our Spirit and bring it forth. This feminine aspect is in our mind, body, emotions. This, the Kundalini Energy which is the Holy Spirit, brings forth the Knowing of our Inner Well of Peace which is the birth of our Holy Spirit. The virgin is one who is fresh, new, undisturbed, unadulterated. Religion has interpreted this virgin, Mary, as unmarried woman devoted to religion. We all are virgin before we take on this Knowing of the Holy Spirit. We are fresh—our Knowing is a Baby, immature, newly born. We are in the stage of being new-born when we become aware of our Holy Spirit.

Christian Mystics compared a virgin to a soul ready to receive God, or in our words, a soul ready to receive the awareness of the Christ, the Holy Spirit, the Kundalini, the Divine Energy.

The virgin is the feminine, the *anima* in Jung's terms, in the psyche of each of us, man or woman. That virgin needs balancing with the masculine within. The marriage of the masculine and feminine may be brief but brings about the birth of our realization of our Inner Christ, that Christ, that Sophia, that Holy Spirit. Our awakening may pass but we shall never forget it, and at some time, in some place, it will come back to our memory and Guide us. Jesus was 30 years old before he started his Mission. Our Holy Spirit birth may lie dormant for 30 years before we recognize it and concentrate on it. Our Mystic Journey is started with consciousness of our Goal.

Let us return to Luke's account of the Annunciation to Mary.

Gabriel told Mary that her cousin Elizabeth, in her old age, had conceived a son and was in her sixth month, although she was said to be barren. Mary went to the house of Zachariah, father of Elizabeth's baby, and greeted Elizabeth. The baby in Elizabeth's womb leaped up in recognition of the baby Mary was carrying. Elizabeth was filled with the Holy Spirit and intuitively knew, and announced to Mary that she was the "mother of my Lord" and "blessed is she who

7

believed that there would be a fulfillment of what was spoken to her by the Lord."

Note that Elizabeth (the inner connection of the soul that declares Truth will come to our consciousness inevitably) greeted Mary as "mother of my Lord" as well as saying that the Lord brought the message to Mary. This Lord was already in Mary but lying safely before birth. This Lord is the Intuitive Knowing that brings to us our birth of awareness of this Golden Gift of who we each are—God the Good. That is what we will finally accept as the Babe matures within us, and we Know "This is my Son, the Beloved, with whom I am well pleased" (Matthew 3:17) applies to us as it did to Jesus at his baptism.

Consciously we shall accept this Knowing. We are all potentially Sons of God. That "Son" is that Holy Spirit which is announced to us in the Annunciation to Mary, our feminine feeling nature. Our feelings are touched so deeply that, like Jesus, the Birth, the Baptism, the Mission, the Crucifixion, the Resurrection, the Ascension will be our Path also.

After Elizabeth's announcement, Mary accepted it and sang praises to the Lord.

> My soul magnifies the Lord, and my spirit rejoices in God my Savior . . ."
> (Luke 1:46, 47)

> For behold, henceforth all generations will call me blessed; for he who is mighty has done great things for me, and holy is his name.
> (Luke 1:48b, 49)

She sang for joy. She knew she had been chosen for a God-given task.

Mary stayed with her cousin three months and returned home to await the birth of Jesus. Elizabeth's baby was John the Baptist who was the forerunner of Jesus. Jesus' Birth and Mission has made all the difference for you and me and this planet.

As mentioned before, Mary has been a very important feminine element in the Catholic Church. Her Assumption, soul and body, into heaven was declared as dogma of the Catholic Church by Pope Pius XII in November 1950 by the Apostolic Constitution and Mary was declared Queen of Heaven and Earth. Carl Jung wrote that this was a balancing of the Trinity into a Quaternity, a symbol of the Self which is central to Jung's philosophy as well as Hindu philosophy. The Self is the Holy Spirit. The Holy Spirit is the feminine aspect in our psyche and Mary being raised to the Queen status balances the Father and Son spoken of in the Trinity. The Feminine is being lifted now all over the Planet.

The Feminine is ascending in both men and women. The Holy Spirit within each is being honored, consciously or unconsciously. The Feminine of caring, loving feeling is ascending. The Feminine of Earth is being repaired, honored and loved. The Feminine, the Holy Spirit, is ascending for many of us who are not connected with the Catholic theology. Lifting Mary to this level has awakened humankind to the need to balance the hearts, bodies and souls of humankind. This will bring Oneness.

Teilhard de Chardin predicted this time, for he said all of humankind was moving toward the Omega Point of Oneness and would reach it some day. The next state of evolution, he said, is the transcendence of consciousness over material and physical limitation. (See his book THE PHENOMENON OF MAN.) That is Ascendancy of the Spirit: the Feminine becomes the Bride of the Bridegroom and we are One. We are closer to Ascendancy than we ever have been. According to Barbara Marx Hubbard we are reaching the point of transcendence from the physical to a Being of Pure Light. This is Ascendancy. (See her book THE REVELATION, OUR CRISIS IS A BIRTH.)

It is Mary, the feminine within us, that brings to birth this Christ, this Holy Child, this Holiest One. We are impregnated by the Holy Spirit, our Holy Spirit, and our Journey toward complete consciousness is begun.

Even though we may have the birth of the awareness of the Christ, it is still a Babe and may face extinction by Herod, the ruling will of the physical. We may go down to Egypt, the realm of substance and body consciousness, but we will return. We may at age twelve, the age Jesus was when he taught in the temple and realized his Mission, have a flash of insight as to our spiritual Path, and then forget it, but eventually it will catch up with us. We may be 30 or 40 years old, or older, before we make a turn around and realize: "This is my son in whom I am well pleased," and then go through the struggle with the world—power, hunger, despair—before we finally start our spiritual Mission. And then, what miracles accrue in our life as we Know and say, "The Father within, he does the work" and "I seek the will of my Father."

Our Path is the Path given us by the Christ, our Kundalini.

9

Now let us turn to the teachings of that Majestic One, Jesus the Christ. His birth into a human body adds credence to the Christian Message of the Christ as the Inner Spirit that is within each of us. That Christ is that Holy Spirit, in all on this earth. We are that Christ. Christ communes with us in our own need.

But first let us discuss the feminine aspect of Jesus as the Christ.

Chapter III

CHRIST AS FEMININE ENERGY

As an introduction I should like to suggest to you the idea of the feminine aspect of Jesus under the names of Wisdom, Sophia, Christ. Due to the patriarchal interpretation of the Gospels and the Church's editing of the original manuscripts, we have lost track of the part that Wisdom, the feminine aspect of the Godhead, has played in the teaching of Jesus the Christ. Since the Christ came in the masculine body, the literalists have made his teaching almost entirely masculine. As a result the feminine traits of Jesus have been lost to our awareness. He was identified in the scripture many times as Son of man.

Let us look at some of the feminine aspects of Jesus Christ.

Many of his statements imply his mothering role, his Wisdom (Sophia) role. For instance, his feeding the thousands—thoroughly feminine activity. His gentleness, his inner-understanding, his compassion—all are feminine traits. Most important is his deep teaching on love, a definite feminine trait. Jesus Christ could be named Jesus-Sophia according to one researcher. Jesus-Holy Spirit might be another title for the Gnostics called the Holy Spirit, Sophia. (See SHE WHO IS by Elizabeth Johnson.) Jesus' reference to the Holy Spirit was definitely in terms of the feminine although the Church has made the Trinity all masculine, which includes the Holy Spirit. Let us look at some scripture on the Holy Spirit of the Christ's teaching.

In John 7:37-39 we have Jesus speaking of quenching thirst, a feminine role:

> On the last day of the feast, the great day, Jesus stood up and proclaimed, "If anyone thirst let him come to me and drink. He who believes in me as the scripture has said, 'Out of his heart shall flow rivers of living water.'" (RSV)

11

But this spake he of the Spirit, which they that believe on him should receive; for the Holy Ghost was not yet given; because that Jesus was not yet glorified. (KJV)

This scripture refers to the Holy Spirit and quenching thirst by living water, the Divine Energy. In Verse 39 the Spirit is the Holy Ghost or the Holy Spirit in the King James Version, the Amplified Version, and the Living New Testament Version of the Scripture.

We have in John 14:26, Jesus Christ's promise to his disciples:

But the Counselor, the Holy Spirit, whom the Father will send in my name, he will teach you all things, and bring to your remembrance all that I have said to you.

My *name* is Christ. The Holy Spirit, the Christ, are the same as the Shekinah in the Kabbalah teaching, Sophia in the Gnostic teaching, Kundalini in Hindu, Shakti in Buddhist teaching. All are feminine. In Hebrew the word for spirit is *ruach*, a feminine term. All of this evidence points to the feminine aspect of the Holy Spirit.

Note that in John 14:26 Jesus says, "the Father will send in my name," the Holy Spirit is the name, the Christ is the name. This is that Inner Grace, a feminine characteristic, within each of us.

I should now like to compare some of the scripture found in the Gospel of John to Wisdom teachings. This would indicate that the writer of John was comparing Jesus' teachings to the Wisdom teachings. We read this as the feminine (Wisdom) speaking through the human and divine Jesus. (I am grateful to John Shelby Spong and his RESCUING THE BIBLE FROM FUNDAMENTALISM for the comparisons.)

Let us start with John 1. The opening verses sound an echo of Genesis 1. We have been taught that a masculine God "created the heavens and the earth." But John says,

In the beginning was the Word; and the Word was with God, and the Word was God. (Verse 1)

Compare this with Proverbs 8:22, 23. Wisdom as "she" is speaking,

Yahweh created me when his purpose first unfolded, before the oldest of his works.

From everlasting, I was firmly set, from the beginning, before earth came into being. (JBV)

And from Sirach 24:9, we read:

From eternity, in the beginning, he created me (Wisdom), and for eternity I shall remain. (JBV)

12

And John 1:2, 3 reads:

> He was in the beginning with God, all things were made through him
> and without him was not anything made that was made.
>
> (The *him* referred to is the Word in John 1:1.)

Compare John 1:14 with Wisdom 7:25:

> And the word became flesh and dwelt among us, full of grace and
> truth; we have beheld his glory, glory as of the only Son from the Fa-
> ther.

From the Apocrypha, Wisdom 7:25:

> She (Wisdom) is a breath of the power of God, pure emanation of
> the glory of the Almighty; hence nothing impure can find a way
> into her.

In John 17:5 we read (Jesus speaking):

> . . . now, Father, glorify thou me in thy own presence with the glory
> which I *had with thee before the world was made*.

Note, "I had with thee before the world was made," and Wisdom
says she was there before the creation
What can we make of this?

Well, it takes a jump over the literal Bible interpretation to allow
the Wisdom literature to be a part of the explanation of the words
of Jesus Christ.

Let us go on—
According to John 6:38:

> For I have come down from heaven, not to do my own will, but the
> will of him who sent me.

Compare with Wisdom 9:17, 18:

> As for your intention, who could have learned it, had you not
> granted Wisdom and sent your holy spirit from above? Thus have
> the paths of those on earth been straightened and men been taught
> what pleases you, and saved by Wisdom.   (JBV)

We all are looking for Divine Truth. Many of us have found it in
teachers, preachers, writings of inspired men and women, the Mystics and from the Holy Bible and Bibles of other religions. But Jesus
taught that Divine Truth was within us as it was within him. He
called it Father, Counselor, Holy Spirit, Higher Power. We call it
intuition, Christ, Self.

In John 17:7, 8 we have the last prayer of Jesus before he was arrested and executed.

13

Now they know that everything that thou hast given me is from thee; for I have given them the words which thou gavest me, and they have received them and know in truth that I came from thee; and they have believed that thou didst send me.

Compare with Wisdom 7:25, 26:

> She is a breath of the power of God, pure emanation of the glory of the Almighty; hence nothing impure can find a way into her. She is a reflection of the eternal light, untarnished mirror of God's active power, image of his goodness.   (JBV)

Wisdom or Christ is from the Most High and It teaches us. This Divine Truth dwells within us.

Jesus called his disciples "little children" in John 13:33. Wisdom calls children "my sons" in Proverbs 8:32. In *Sirach 6:18, Wisdom addresses "my son" and directs him to "cultivate instruction." And last, in comparing John's teaching and the Wisdom teaching we find that Wisdom, the Christ, pervaded and penetrated all things just as the Kundalini energy does.

> For within her (wisdom) is a spirit intelligent, holy, unique, manifold, subtle, active, invulnerable, benevolent, sharp, irresistible, beneficent, loving to man, steadfast, dependable, unperturbed, almighty, all-surveying, penetrating, all intelligent, pure and most subtle spirit; for Wisdom is quicker to move than any motion; she is pure, she pervades and permeates all things.   (Wisdom 7:22-24)

That is the Christ. That is the Holy Spirit. That is the Kundalini. That is the feminine aspect of God.

The Christ said in John 14:23 and 15:4 that he inhabited those who believed in him and he gave them the Holy Spirit. He breathed on them and gave them the Holy Spirit. (John 20:22)

Christ was and is Wisdom, Holy Spirit, Divine Love and *she* gave It to the disciples and gives It to all of us.

Now that we have been introduced to the feminine aspect of Jesus through John's teaching and the Wisdom scriptures, let us go forward and read the feminine, Sophia, into the Christ's words of Wisdom. Sometimes I may change the pronoun relating to Jesus, "he," to "she." Just let that choice sink into your consciousness and feel your Intuitive reaction. You may be surprised!

*Sirach is the same as Ecclesiasticus.

14

Chapter IV

THE MARRIAGE AT CANA OF GALILEE

John 2:1-11

This is considered Jesus' first miracle by some Bible scholars. It has been interpreted to mean whatever the speaker or writer needed in order to demonstrate a point. As we know, Jesus performed many miracles. A miracle according to the dictionary is an event in the physical world deviating from the known laws of nature. According to Charles Fillmore, miracles take place as a result of the operation of a higher, unknown law. Jesus functioned in that kind of law.

I shall interpret this miracle from the viewpoint of the Mystical Marriage—the Ecstasy of Oneness. The weddings or marriages recorded in the Bible carry this secret esoteric meaning. We will come to others later.

The account is that on the third day there was a marriage in Cana of Galilee. Jesus, his mother and his disciples attended. Weddings in those days were a village celebration. When there was no more wine, Jesus' mother told him. He, at first rejected her unspoken suggestion that he do something about it. Then he told the servants to fill with water the six stone jars which had formerly held water for the Jewish rites of purification. The water then became wine. They took some of the wine to the steward of the feast and he was surprised that the wine was better than they had drunk at the beginning of the celebration. The last verse of the account reads:

> This, the first of his signs (miracles), Jesus did at Cana in Galilee, and manifested his glory; and his disciples believed in Him.
>
> (John 2:11)

15

The glory of Jesus was the high level of vibration of his body, mind, and spirit.

Cana symbolizes a reed, a rod, a rule. Immediately, if you have followed my writing, you will see this brings to mind the spine up which the Kundalini flows.* Galilee symbolizes rolling energy or soul energy. So our setting is ready—the Kundalini will move up the spine, fill the six jars (chakras) and the Mystic Marriage will come forth.

The Bible does not tell us how Jesus performed this Miracle. We know that once we are in unity with the Divine Presence our very thoughts are capable of performing miracles. It would appear that this was how Jesus changed the water into wine. Our thoughts affect everything and everyone around us when we have reached this high level of Oneness.

The Mystic Marriage is the culmination of the body, mind, soul and feelings being filled with the Divine Energy of the Serpent Fire. Esoterically we have here the setting for the combination of water and fire which will bring us to high Ecstasy.

The mother of Jesus has been identified by some scholars as symbolic of the Divine Feminine or Wisdom. It is Wisdom or the Kundalini that directs us to fulfill our needs for the Mystic Marriage. Or we could see the Christ as Wisdom, Sophia. In any case, the feminine gave the orders to the servants (lower nature) to do whatever the Holy one, the Christ, told them to do.

The lower nature can only provide water for physical needs, for cleansing, for keeping the physical body alive. This Divine Energy is also used for generation. The lower nature serves the higher nature when the Christ is present and regeneration takes place.

The disciples were there and symbolize our human faculties, our human senses not yet Christed. They are present at the Mystic Marriage but are merely spectators.

The six stone water pots are the six chakras which are filled with the water of physical life until the Divine Energy changes the contents to Spirit—to wine. These six chakras are filled and then the seventh chakra explodes in Ecstasy with the coming together of the masculine and the feminine in the Mystic Marriage. The stone pots must be filled first.

The water in the pots had been used for the rite of cleansing. We must also clean these chakras by the Silence, by prayer, by

* Addendum

16

right-eous-ness before the wine (Spirit) can be freed. Wine is also a symbol of the libido—the Divine Energy.

The steward of the feast is our own intellect guiding our celebration of the Spirit. We are still conscious. The steward directs the mind to allow this to happen. The intellect (masculine) is often disinterested in the lack, but the feminine always knows our need. The feminine is our soul and it is trying to reach Oneness with the Godhead.

Jesus The Christ is silent while the six stone pots are being filled. With his deep knowledge of the power of his thought projecting the Divine Energy into the water, he changed the water into wine and the Marriage feast went forward to completion. In his silence he was preparing.

At first, the Christ seemed to reject the suggestion by the feminine (his mother) to do something about the lack of wine. Perhaps he did not think he was ready to perform miracles. But, as with us, we will finally carry out the wishes of the feminine.

Christ is our own Inner Knowing that there is something more to our spiritual fulfillment than physical use of the Life Energy. We have a Divine Knowing within, our Holy Spirit, that moves us higher and higher toward our own Mystical Marriage.

It is suggested in Verse 11 that the Christ manifested her glory, or her power, at other incidents of Cana in Galilee. This we shall look forward to as we study her miracles further. She brought soul ecstasy to many. (She/her is Jesus-Sophia.)

Wine, Life Eternal, Divine Energy is within each of us. To become conscious of it we shall follow the teachings of Jesus the Christ.

Corinne Heline, one of my most important Teachers, has this to say:

> At the Mystic Marriage the glory of white light in the soul of the mystic is united in ruby splendor in the soul of the occultist; water is transmuted into wine. (VOLUME V, p. 116)

And Emma Curtis Hopkins says:

> This marriage in Cana was the outward picture of the primal union or marriage of Jesus Christ with Spirit.
> (BIBLE INTERPRETATIONS SERIES ONE, p. 4)

Since this was Jesus' first miracle it may indicate his first awareness of his Power through his Holy Spirit. As we know, many what

17

we would call miracles, were performed by him. When we have reached our Highest State we, too, can perform miracles with the high vibration of the Kundalini. In fact, when we are reaching for unity with the Godhead, many miracles accrue along our Way. We need to recognize them as coming from the Spirit of Truth.

Chapter V

CLEANSING THE TEMPLE

John 2:13-25

This account of Jesus' cleansing the temple in Jerusalem is recorded in all the Gospels.

In John 2:12 it is said that Jesus went to Capernaum with his mother, his brothers and his disciples. They stayed there a few days. Capernaum symbolizes comfort, compassion, harmony. Here Jesus stayed with his mother, that Divine Energy which gives birth to our Christ consciousness. Then he went to Jerusalem (the dwelling place of peace). To go to peace is to go to the foundation of the Christ Way through meditation, the Silence.

There was celebrating of the Passover going on in the Temple, and the merchants were selling sheep, oxen and pigeons for sacrifice. Also, the money changers, who were interested in profit, were there and were accosted by Jesus. He turned over their tables with the coins on them. He addressed those who were selling pigeons to take away the "things, for you shall not make my Father's house a house of trade." (The Jews believed that God resided in the Temple.) The Jews protested and asked Jesus by what authority he did this. Jesus answered, "Destroy this temple and in three days I will raise it up." (Verse 19) Verse 21 explains this: "But he spoke of the temple of his body." The following verses report that many believed in his name and the last line of the chapter reads, "for he himself knew what was in man." So what was *in* man?

Taken literally, many preachers and teachers have used this incident as proof that Jesus the Christ was not above anger and the destroying of others' property. Those who believe they are following Jesus' example often use this incident to prove that their own expression of anger at someone who does not agree with them is totally acceptable because Jesus did it.

This incident was mentioned several times by the Jewish authorities to support their decision to stop Jesus' teaching. Especially his remark that he could destroy the temple and rebuild it in three days. Even while Jesus was on the cross many derided him with this statement. (See Matthew 26:61.) This remark was very important for his future.

We do not know whether Verse 19 "in three days I will raise it up" supports the teaching of the Resurrection, but it does not matter really, for we shall approach it from an esoteric viewpoint.

The idea that he was speaking of his body was underscored by I Corinthians 6: 19-20b which, from Paul referring to this verse, reads:

> Do you not know that your body is a temple of the Holy Spirit within you, which you have from God? . . . So glorify God in your body.

Three days has been used throughout the Old and New Testament as the time it takes for sacrifice, for cleansing the mind and body (Esther 4:16), before making a journey, before fighting a battle. Heline reports Initiates had to remain three days in the Secret Place in Egypt to complete Initiation Rites. Perhaps Jesus was referring to some of this secret knowledge. In any case, the Pharisees took his statement literally since they were into logic and intellectual Law.

Paul says that the body is the temple of the Holy Spirit and how often we are guilty of desecrating that temple. Preparation of that temple is necessary—cleansing of that temple is necessary—if we are to reach the consciousness level of regeneration. Some teaching requires that celibacy be practiced to cleanse the temple of the lust of sex—that could also be a cleansing on a human level.

The body includes not only the physical but also the mind, the feeling nature, the unconscious, the conscious. In some accounts of this incident Jesus says, "It is written, 'My house shall be called a house of prayer,' but ye have made it a den of thieves." (Matthew 21:13 KJV) God's house is our conscious realization of Who we are, and it is a House of prayer when we step on the Path.

Awareness has the conscious and unconscious of the psyche and the unconscious has often been stuffed with memories of so many negative thoughts and experiences that our conscious mind has

20

been desecrated in the temple of the Spirit. The temple is our body *and* consciousness. The thoughts need cleansing also.

The Scripture reports that the Christ, with a cord, drove the negative robbers away. This cord, from the esoteric view, is the spine up which the Divine Energy, the Sophia or Christ, cleanses our body and our thoughts. When we let this Divine Energy flow, we are cleansed of our animal-like behavior as well as our concentration on the outer physical.

No outer authority—no masculine power can do this for us. We must each do it for our own regeneration. When Jesus said he could raise the temple in three days, I suggest that he was alluding to the three days that are necessary for us to overcome death. It was raising up his Light body from death that he was speaking of.

Eastern religionists teach that the Spirit is attached to the physical body for three days after the body becomes inert, a state which we call death. Therefore, they recommend that if the body is to be cremated a period of three days should pass before that is done.

Cleansing of the body for three days may also relate to our nutrition. It is most important that we cooperate with the movement of the Spirit by eating nutritious foods, drinking pure water, exercising and blessing our bodies. It is also important to help that Kundalini movement by fasting, prayer, meditation, positive thoughts, and celebrating our Oneness.

Many who are on the Path to Enlightenment do not realize the importance of cleaning the shadow out of the unconscious, although this is becoming well known now. The shadow in our thinking and feeling, as a result of past thoughts or actions, brings a block to the free movement of that Divine Spirit. The *status quo* (the Jews) will often get in our way and will argue with our cleansing of our unconscious. This, too, must be freed from animal-like propensities; from fear that may motivate us to give our whole life to accumulating materialism and to being attached to relationships and things. These shadows must be cleansed—not by covering up, but by deep inner work through contemplation, dream analysis or other therapy. Many resist this because they are afraid to look at their shadow. All of this must be sacrificed or it will defile our temple, mind, body, soul and heart.

Many are able to cleanse their unconscious by meditating and listening to the "still small voice" as did Elijah before he went out to do his great work. Father Thomas Keating recommends this method. (See Chapter 9 in his OPEN MIND, OPEN HEART.) However it is done, know that cleansing is a must. Our temple cannot be pure until this is done.

The Christ brings about this cleansing for us.

I am sure that the next hour the sheep, oxen, pigeons and money changers returned to the Temple, for the Jews were not convinced that Jesus' teaching was from the Messiah. His Sophia led him to teach this deep truth by use of physical symbols. It is our choice, after the cleansing, whether we follow through and quit desecrating our Holy Temple.

Our feminine Energy, our Christ will act and we will be cleansed when It is flowing freely and clearly throughout our consciousness. Our three days may extend to three decades or three lifetimes or more, but it will happen. Our Soul demands it.

It is in Jerusalem, the city of peace, that we find our Joy. The temple of our body and consciousness is at peace when it has been cleansed. Peace is our perfect habitation, and this teaching gives us Guidance to that Place. The Spirit, at home in our Temple, does its work. The cord filled with Light does its work.

Jesus-Sophia did the work and has given us our perfect example.

Chapter VI

NICODEMUS, THE PHARISEE

John 3:1-16

Very briefly the account says that Nicodemus, a Pharisee and ruler of the Jews, came to talk to Jesus at night, ostensibly so no one would see him.

He gave Jesus his "due" by remarking that he had observed the signs he, Jesus, had done and that God must be with him for him to do them. Jesus' reply seems remote from the answer that Nicodemus may have expected. He said,

> Truly, truly, I say to you, unless one is born anew (from above), he cannot see the kingdom of God. (John 3:3)

Nicodemus from his Pharisaical mind-set inquired as to how one could be born again if he was old. This was from his intellectual, reasoning mind. Jesus then replied,

> Truly, truly, I say to you, unless one is born of water and the Spirit, he cannot enter the kingdom of God. (John 3:5)

Then Jesus continued to explain that there is birth of the flesh and birth of the Spirit; that the Spirit moves like the wind and we do not know where it comes from or where it goes, and thus it is for everyone born of the Spirit. (Spirit, wind, breath are synonymous.)

Nicodemus did not understand yet. Jesus suggested he was closed minded and could not believe. In Verse 13 he explains:

> "No one has ascended into heaven but he who descended from heaven, the Son of man."

This term *Son of man* will be discussed further on.

Verses 14, 15 gives us a definite clue as to what he was teaching as he reminds this Jew that as Moses "lifted up the serpent in the wilderness, so must the Son of man be lifted up, that whoever believes in him may have eternal life."

Evidently Jesus made an impact on Nicodemus, for in John 7:50, 51 Nicodemus told the chief priests and Pharisees who were trying to arrest Jesus, that a hearing should be allowed Jesus before he was arrested. Also, in John 19:39 when Jesus' body was being prepared for burial, Nicodemus brought myrrh and aloes and these were used in the burial cloth.

Now let us get to this Scripture for our own teaching.

First, let us discuss being "born again" since this seemed a most troublesome concept for Nicodemus and is for many today. Because Nicodemus (the ruling tendency of the mind, left brain thinking) heard Jesus' answer from a literal standpoint, he saw this idea as ridiculous. How could one who is grown enter his/her mother and be born again. Jesus explained, but if Nicodemus' ego was still refuting the answer he would not "get" the message.

Being born of water can symbolize being born from the water of the birthing mother, or it can mean being cleansed, some believe, through baptism in water, and see this cleansing as part of the human evolution to higher consciousness. Our physical life depends on water, and as we live that life we may go through some experiences that soil the awareness of our Spiritual destiny. The physical life of water is necessary to help us to be "born anew."

Others would see water as the unconscious. The unconscious cleansing is also necessary. Cleansing the unconscious opens us to consciousness of who we are and then we are "born again" in the Spirit.

Now, why would we want to be "born anew or again"?

Nicodemus did not ask how he could enter the Kingdom of God. Why did Jesus emphasize that in answer to Nicodemus' question.

The Christ knows, our Christ knows, that our greatest aim is to find Oneness with the Universal Energy we call God. Much of Jesus' teaching was on how to enter the Kingdom of Heaven or Kingdom of God. He knew the deepest desire of each of those he spoke to, and his words find a place in our deep longing for that place of Bliss, Ecstasy, Peace, Joy, Love, called Heaven. It is very unconscious with most of us, and we try to fill that longing with things that are material and with relationships, but nothing suffices until we are "born again."

To be "born again" is to start our life out on a new Quest. When we are "born anew" we turn to our Spirit, our Spirit Mother, for our

Joy and our Fulfillment. We turn to the inner Holy Spirit for our Guidance. Oh, we may not do this at first, for we are still babes, but as we mature we will realize that our Goal is that Mystic Marriage, that Kingdom of Heaven which can be had here and now. Jesus said it was within us. (Luke 17:21) His Guidance for Nicodemus is our Guidance also.

So to be "born anew" is to awaken to the conscious realization of our Holy Spirit which is that Holy Spark from the Godhead. It is always there and we become aware of It when we are "born again;" and this experience may be a silent realization within our Inner Knowing. This new birth will change our life, our choices, our goals, our living. We will become a new person, a new Being in our Christ.

This Holy Spirit or Holy Spark leads us, if we follow, to the realization of the flowing Spirit within our body and consciousness. This is just the beginning. We will continue to mature, we will meditate, we will feel that Spinal Fire awakening and we will let it open all of our chakras until we are in Bliss and Ecstasy beyond any such experience that sexual activity, alcohol, drugs or physical pleasure could bring. The "born again" phase of our Journey is just a beginning. The result of that great birth will take us to such Joy that we never dreamed was possible. Our loss of worry, fear and negative emotions will come on gradually, and we will eventually rest in the Will of the I AM and be complete in Oneness with It.

We must note that Nicodemus was a Pharisee symbolizing one who depends on the power and thought of the intellect. The Pharisee followed outer Law and did not go within for Guidance.

Nicodemus, who was aware of Jesus' acts, came out of the darkness, or at night, to question him.

We are all in spiritual darkness as long as we depend on our ego, our intellect, to live our life, to direct us in our life, and many times we do not allow others to know of this Quest for spiritual insight. We keep it secret for we are afraid of the criticism of our peers, our family, our associates, and it takes an act of courage to break away from a religious teaching that does not fit any more. But if we do, and look closely, we shall see miracles occurring in our life and may wonder if this is God caring for us. Eventually we will search and find the answer, and then we are on the Way to the Kingdom of Heaven—our Oneness with God.

Many times this New Birth comes on us unexpectedly. We may not recognize the Grace of God, the Spirit moving in our mundane experiences, but that Still Small Voice can speak volumes in our unconscious and seep through into our conscious mind. Dreams are a great conveyer of this Truth. The Spirit moves at Its own behest, and later we marvel at the beginning of our being "born again."

Jesus said in John 3:8: "The wind blows where it wills . . . so it is with every one who is born of the Spirit."

Jesus then tells Nicodemus how he can be sure of the message—by *knowing* and by *seeing*. But we often block this with our intellect and the outer Law. It is by that Inner Knowing, that experiencing within our Self, that we are "born again." No one teacher can convince us without our own experience within the Self.

Verse 13 introduces us to the phrase "Son of man." We shall dwell on this at length, for it is a teaching that we must understand in terms of my Thesis.

In the Book of Ezekiel there is much reference to son of man or Son of man. In Jesus' speaking he often used the term "Son of man" which many have believed referred to him exclusively. I should like to suggest alternative meanings for the term, as I believe it applies to each of us personally.

Paramahansa Yogananda, the great Hindu guru who came to the United States to teach the combination of the Christ teaching and the Hindu teaching, says that "Son of man" refers to the physical body and the astral body of Jesus as well as each one of us. (THE SECOND COMING OF CHRIST, page 146) The astral body is the body of Light surrounding the physical body when the Kundalini is active.

Other definitions I have gleaned from my study includes one from John Shelby Spong in RESCUING THE BIBLE FROM FUNDAMENTALISM in which he writes that Son of man is one who acts as God's agent and with God's authority. Edward F. Edinger writes that the Son of man is the same as the Christ, the Self, in his book THE BIBLE AND THE PSYCHE. Elaine Pagels in her popular book, THE GNOSTIC GOSPELS, indicates that Son of man means, according to the Gnostics, The Son of Anthropos (humanity) and is the spiritual essence of human being. And Charles Fillmore, co-founder of Unity School, explains in the METAPHYSICAL BIBLE DICTIONARY that; "Son of man is the real I AM but limited by thought. Jesus is Son of man—human and Divine. Son is the Absolute within each of us." (page 626)

All of these point us to the possibility of accepting the Son of man as that Holy Spirit (masculinized by the Church's Trinity) dwelling in each of us. "Son," capitalized, designates that Divine Energy, the Spark of the Godhead, that indwells us all; and "man" refers to the physical part of us, to the intellect, and to our very human characteristics. This Son "comes down" and dwells within us. We are conscious of it on different levels—mental, mystical and finally Absolute. Jesus Christ knew it on the Absolute level and It came through his words and works as the Father. This brings us to John 3:13:

> No one has ascended into heaven but he who descended from heaven, the Son of man.

That Son is in each of us. That Son is the Holy Spirit descended into matter. That Son ascends into Heaven consciousness as we lift up the Spirit within our consciousness, up our spinal column into all the chakras, and this happens not by conscious manipulation, but by the Grace of the Creator. But first we cause it to descend from its heavenly state through our humanness. Then It will ascend back to that consciousness of the Absolute. Each then becomes the Son of God. Jesus was living his life as an example for all of us. He said we could do what he had done and more. We are all Sons/Daughters of God and will become conscious of that Truth eventually. Then we shall reach the Kingdom of Heaven. But we must be "born anew" to make that ascent, as Jesus taught.

Let us now discuss John 3:14, 15:

> And as Moses lifted up the serpent in the wilderness so must the Son of man be lifted up, that whoever believes in him may have eternal life.

The account of Moses making the brazen serpent, putting it on a pole, and lifting it up is dealt with in Numbers 21:9.

The people were cured of poisonous serpent bites (misuse of Divine Energy) when their eyes were lifted to the Serpent Energy held high, having risen through the spine (pole) for regeneration.

Jesus uses Old Testament analogy often. He says here that the Son of man must be lifted up if one is to have eternal life. Eternal life is often equated by Jesus with the Kingdom of Heaven. The Serpent Energy, the Divine Energy, is our Spark of the Godhead which has descended into human form. This Spark is often called the breath. In Greek, spirit and breath mean the same. In Hinduism and Buddhism, spirit is breath or wind, as Jesus pointed out in John 3:8. The Paraclete (Greek for Comforter, Holy Spirit); Ruach (the Spirit in Hebrew and feminine); the Shekinah for the Kabbalist; Sophia for the Gnostics must be lifted up. The same is the Son (Spirit) in humanity.

Since Eternal Life and Kingdom of Heaven are synonymous terms, Jesus is repeating the phrase "unless one is born anew, he cannot see the kingdom of Heaven" by saying that the Son of man must be lifted up to have Eternal Life.

The Serpent Energy lifted up for regeneration brings us to the Kingdom state of consciousness, to Enlightenment. Jesus is our primary example.

John 3:16-21 is not universally accepted as being spoken by Jesus at this event. However, since John 3:16 is such an important scripture to so many, I should like to discuss it from my perspective.

> For God so loved the world that he gave his only Son, that whoever believes in him should not perish but have eternal life.

God loves us. We are in the world and we have this Spark of Love within us and when we believe in That and "lift it up" we shall have Eternal Life. The Divine Energy is the only Son.

"God so loved the world" catches our consciousness. God loves the world. God is not waiting to punish us, to send us to Hell. God loves the world and all in it.

God's only Son is the Spirit of Truth which abides in us. That Son is ever with us. Our task is to recognize that Holy Feminine by translating Son to Mother or Daughter. We know that when we believe on Her we shall have Life Eternal. In Jesus' words:

> But the Counselor, the Holy Spirit, whom the Father will send in my name, (she) will teach you all things and bring to your remembrance all that I have said to you.
>
> (John 14:26)
> (parenthesis mine)

Thus we have John 3:16 as it applies to each individual Journey.

Further on in this discourse on the Son, we have reference to light. Verse 21 refers to coming to the light. Light is another word for the Divine Energy.

> But he who does what is true comes to the light that it may be clearly seen that his deeds have been wrought in God.

The light is God. Light is within us as the Holy Spirit.

In consciousness, inner experience, the still small voice, is the Son, Divine Child, and is of God. Jesus said, "Blessed are the peacemakers for they shall be called the children of God." (Matthew 5:9 KJV) Peace is our inheritance and we are Sons (children) of God. We should not try to restrain the Spirit. It goes where it will. We breathe It in and then release It. The Spirit is our life and we release It to roam throughout the experiences of our life. We serve, we bless, we pray and we are blessed, for when we are born of the Spirit It takes over our life and we go forth to serve God and humanity. The Spirit is free. We must not limit Its movement by our Pharisaical intellect. It is a free gift.

God so loves us that He gives us our Holy Spirit that when we believe in Her we shall have Eternal Life/Kingdom of Heaven. Thus it is that Jesus gave us one of his most important teachings, so that we may know about being "born anew."

Nicodemus, a ruler over the Pharisees (religious belief based on intellect) came to ask Jesus questions from spiritual darkness (he came at night). Later he was convinced enough to question the religious authorities' treatment of Jesus and he brought spices for Jesus' embalming. He was "born again." His questioning brought us a most important teaching from Jesus, our Elder Brother/Sister.

Chapter VII

THE SAMARITAN WOMAN
AT THE WELL

John 4:3-42

The Woman at the Well is nearly always written or spoken about in terms of Jesus' great love and lack of prejudice, but it carries a much deeper message as we shall learn as we go through it.

Jesus and his disciples were traveling from Judea (praise Jehovah) to Galilee (manifestation of Divine Energy or rolling Energy). They chose to travel through Samaria (watch tower, intellect). The Samaritans were not acceptable to the Jews for they were from Jewish and Assyrian parentage. They did not worship the God of the Temple in Jerusalem. They were tinged with Baal worship.

They came to a town, Sychar (confused state of mind, idolatry), where Jacob's well was. Jacob symbolizes intellect. Jesus sat down by the well to rest while his disciples went into town to obtain food. A woman approached the well to draw water. Jesus asked her for a drink. She was greatly surprised as Jews never even acknowledged that a Samaritan was around; especially a Jewish man would not speak to a Samaritan woman, but Jesus honored women all through his ministry. So she asked him how he, a Jew, could ask her, a Samaritan woman, for a drink.

I must say that the first scene carries much teaching for us from a deep psychological/spiritual level.

The woman symbolizes the feminine nature of each of us. The Soul is feminine. Our Soul is often searching for the water, the Spirit, to quiet Its thirst. For the feminine to be asked to give some water to the masculine is not unusual. What is unusual is that the masculine asks the feminine for something it needs. The masculine is the ego. And the ego, when strong within us, has no use for the

31

feminine soul. It, the ego, usually ignores the feminine soul. But when our ego is in need, when it is weary and thirsty for it knows not what, the feminine, the Grace of God, will appear and the ego being momentarily weary, will turn to the feminine, the soul, for help in its need.

But let us go on.

Jesus answered her:

> "If you knew the gift of God, and who it is that is saying to you, 'Give me a drink,' you would have asked him and he would have given you living water." (Verse 10)

Now the Woman was really surprised. She pointed out that he did not have any vessel to draw water from the well. She asked where he would get this living water.

He answered her by pointing out that everyone who drinks of the water from the well would thirst again, but whoever drank of the water he shall give would never thirst. The water "will become in him a spring of water welling up to eternal life." (Verse 14) Eternal life, a place in consciousness that does not require us to return to this vale of tears. We will be at One in the Godhead and will not need to return to this physical life for more cleansing. We will be Home, in the Kingdom of Heaven.

Eternal life! That for which all humankind longs!

She still did not understand. Her first thought was that she would not have to come to the well again to draw and carry the water. (This was of course true as the intellect lets go and the intuition, supplied by the "living water," would take care of her needs.) She asked him to give the "living water" to her. She did not realize what she was asking for. Living water is that Kundalini Energy.

But she was tested. Jesus asked her to go call her husband. She said she had none. Then Jesus pointed out that she had had five husbands and was now living with a man out of wedlock. She was honest—a most important personality characteristic if we are to receive that "living water." She did not deny her past or present conditions.

She was impressed by his psychic ability. She called him a prophet. She then pointed out the difference between her people worshiping on Mt. Gerizim (the Samaritan temple was there) and his people worshiping in Jerusalem. Her race consciousness of intellect argued.

32

Our intellect often calls up argument when we are overwhelmed with Truth. Our intellect wants to argue. Jesus pointed out that they worshiped a false God, for salvation was from the Jews.

The salvation he spoke of was the coming of the Messiah from the Jewish race. Then he told her that neither place would be the place of worship for her, for she would worship in spirit and in truth. This is what the Father wants, he said.

God is spirit, and those who worship him must worship in spirit and truth. (Verse 24)

He was pointing out that God was not to be found in a mountain to worship, or in a temple, but worship must be centered within on Spirit and Truth.

She was confused. She said she knew the Messiah (Christ) was coming and would teach the people all they should know.

Jesus answered: "I who speak to you am he." (Verse 26)

That "I am" is very important in Jesus' teaching. We shall go into that in Chapter VIII.

It was the Christ, the Spirit, coming through the consciousness of Jesus that was speaking to the Woman. Truth comes from the Inner Self.

This was too much for her! She knew he spoke the Truth. I believe he had given her this Spirit through his speaking to her, his looking at her. The "living water" had been passed on to her unconscious and she was becoming conscious of It.

The "living water" has been interpreted by many through the ages as symbolizing the Fountain of Life, the Holy Spirit, the Christ. Water is feminine in Taoism, the yin. It also symbolizes the unconscious, intuitive Wisdom.

Thomas Keating says in his THE MYSTERY OF CHRIST (page 92): "The Spirit is the stream of living water which wells up in those who believe."

Yogananda, from his THE SECOND COMING OF CHRIST (page 156) says: "Eternal Bliss in God is where we find the living water within, and afterwards we are never thirsty for mortal desires or mortal life." (Paraphrased)

There is no account which indicates that Jesus gave her the "living water" baptism, but he got her complete attention when he told her about her husbands and the unmarried state of her living. At that second, or instant, she received his offer of "living water." She had asked for it previously. The disciple must open to receive.

· We cannot separate Jesus' acts from the belief and practice of religionists for centuries before his advent. Shaktipat, or the awakening of Kundalini within a disciple, had been practiced by the Hindus as well as by practitioners of must religions. This arousing of the Divine Energy can come through touch, word, look or thought of the teacher or enlightened person to the Seeker. The laying on of hands on various parts of the body—the third eye, or the heart, or at the base of the spine—will also bring it alive. Jesus did this for the Woman at the well. He looked, thought and spoke the word to the Woman.

Taking symbolism further, because the masculine and feminine must become One in order for us to enjoy Eternal Life, the feminine must often be awakened by the masculine and vice versa. It depends on the personality type of the individual, according to Jung. The intellectual type often starts their Journey by thought control. This the metaphysicians teach. The intuitive type who are more feminine will often have a spiritual experience which leads them to trying to understand the experience by reading, talking, thinking. In the case of the Woman, she was more intellectual being Samaritan, while Jesus was the Spirit opening her to a higher level of Knowing, and she would never thirst again for peace, harmony, spirit.

Jesus said in John 7:38: "He who believes in me, as the scripture has said, 'Out of his heart shall flow rivers of living water.'" This living water is love, is Bliss, is the Holy Spirit that fills the whole being of the Seeker. "Believe in me" refers to the Christ, to the I AM, not to the physical Jesus.

The woman was overwhelmed. She left her water jar (she did not need water coming from the intellect, the well in Samaria, anymore) and ran to the city to tell the people that this man had read her past. She asked, "Can this be the Christ?" She was not fully convinced. Things had happened so fast. Although the Spirit was aroused within her, she was still tied to the intellect—her people. It would take time for her to accept.

The people went to the well to see Jesus and many believed in him because of the woman's (feminine) testimony. They were attracted to his psychic ability. Many of us start our Journey from the psychic realm. The intellect is searching for an explanation of so-called miracles and thus we are opened to the Word. The account says that Jesus and his disciples stayed two days and taught the people. Then the people confessed that it was no longer the woman's testimony, but their own experience that caused them to believe that Jesus was "the Savior of the world."

That is how Truth is spread. The testimony of one, the Divine experience of that one, makes the testimony acceptable to others. We begin by believing the account or teaching of another. Eventually we have the experience of our Self.

The "living water" was given without price. The Christ within, the Word, teaches us and we become whole. With more teaching and more experiencing we evolve in consciousness.

Matthew Fox, in his book on the sermons of Meister Eckhart, the great fourteenth century mystic, quotes Eckhart as saying:

> We read about a women who received a gift from Christ. The first gift which God gives is the Holy Spirit; in that gift, God gives all of his gifts. That is "the living water, whomever I give this to will never thirst again." This water is grace and light and springs up in the soul and rises within and presses upward and leaps up into eternity.
>
> (BREAKTHROUGH, p. 371)

Let us not leave the disciples behind, for Jesus gave us a wonderful teaching through his conversation with them.

After the woman left they had brought something back from the city to eat and suggested to Jesus that he eat. His reply was that "My food is to do the will of him who sent me, and to accomplish his work." He knew his Purpose and would carry it out until the end.

He needed no food or drink after his high experience with teaching the Woman. His "living water" was flowing like a Fountain. When we are doing our spiritual work our body does not require so much food, drink, rest. It is filled with the Energy of the All-Filling Presence and does not need the food it may have needed previously.

He further taught them that when an opportunity comes for us to teach, to lift up the "living water" in another, we must do it. "I tell you, lift up your eyes, and see how the fields are already white for harvest." (Verse 35) "Look up" is a major teaching of Emma Curtis Hopkins. (See HIGH MYSTICISM.)

Our purpose, when we are called by the Spirit to do a work, is to do it here and now. It is not for us to wait until we are in the right place at the right time according to our own intellectual choice.

When we realize we are sent for this Purpose we must give the good word, the baptism, the example of the Spirit flowing. Each person must be dealt with on an individual basis and not as a member of a group.

That is what is happening to many now. They have left the church, the synagogue, the temple and are finding their own Holy Spirit through meditation, prayer, reading the Bible and other books that feed their need. The desire to KNOW, to experience that Spirit within drives them to Seek, and these are open to the teaching of one who has found the answer.

We sow and another reaps. We reap what another sows. We are all One and as we follow the teachings of the Christ we will learn that the One I AM is within us all and waiting for our attention.

The Gift of God is Eternal Life and as we listen to our Christ and follow, thus it will be. The Christ said to the woman: "The water that I shall give him (her) will become in him (her) a spring of water welling up to eternal life." (Verse 14)

We have that Fountain. We are that Fountain, and we share our Divine Presence with Jesus the Christ and all our sisters and brothers. This is the Spirit and the Truth. This is Eternal Life.

Many times when we are in a high state of praising Jehovah (Judah) and are going to Galilee (rolling Divine Energy) we may go through the land of the intellect (Samaria) and worship the outer God, not the inner Spirit. Thus the Woman at the Well has taught us. The Christ comes to us by the Grace of the Author of Life. We are fed by that Grace.

Chapter VIII

I AM,
THE DIVINE ENERGY

It is imperative that we discuss this phrase, I AM, or as many understand it, The Word. Much of traditional interpretation of I AM has been founded on the words of Jesus as a historical figure. It is so often forgotten that Jesus, the man, was speaking from his Inner Christ, the I AM. When we study his teachings from this plane of Knowing, we get an entirely different understanding. Our intuition tells us clearly that I AM is that Christ within each of us. That Christ is the Spirit of Truth, is the Spirit that invades all. I AM is the eternal Word.

John 1:1: "In the beginning was the Word, and the Word was with God, and the Word was God." Thus, is the I AM.

We have struggled, all religions, to name, to describe the Godhead. It has been given various nomenclatures by the Christians, such as: God, Mighty Omnipresence, Truth, Father of All, One I AM, High Watch, Father. None of these can be defined to the satisfaction of all. We have used God as a name to be understood, but our Judeo/Christian teaching has made It masculine, while the mystics have claimed that the Godhead, above all and in all, is neuter. Meister Eckhart gave many definitions of the Godhead which, among other teachings, got him into trouble with Catholic authorities. We are freer now but yet find it impossible to define It to the satisfaction of all who studied It.

The other religions of the world have their own name for this Eternal Energy. Some of them are Brahm, Parabrahman, Tao, The Buddha, Allah, Rama, Shiva, Ganesh. All names are an attempt to give their followers a title that can be used in prayer, speaking and writing.

37

Some of the definitions of God given by scholars, mystics, and Seekers of the Way are interesting. These definitions somewhat define the Absolute to our intellect.

Some of them are for the Judeo/Christian follower: Eternal Word; I AM; Being or Be-ness; He Who Is; I am who I am; I am He (who) causes to be; I AM who Am; Self; It Is; Spirit of Man; Spirit of God; Christ; Father.

As we study the words of Jesus in the Book of John we will come up with many more terms related to the Highest One, the Ain Soph. (See definition in Glossary.)

Now, why, you may be asking, is this so important? We know what I AM indicates, you may be thinking. Why belabor this?

I should like to answer your questions by turning to the book by John Shelby Spong, RESCUING THE BIBLE FROM FUNDAMENTALISM.

On page 204 he starts with the beginning of this Biblical phrase, and refers to Exodus 3:13ff.

Spong reviews the account of Moses asking God's name. He then writes:

> The name of God was in some way related to the verb "to be." This was the message of Exodus revealed in the call of Moses. God was being, the ground of being, the fullness of being, the sum of being, being itself. God is. Of this God it could be said that "the eternal and complete 'I' shares, undergirds, and affirms the eternal and complete world that is." "I AM" was their way of saying this, of describing the indescribable. "I AM" was God's name.

The Voice from the Burning Bush (Moses' Inner Voice) told Moses to save his people, the Israelites. Moses questioned who he should say had sent him. The Voice answered "I AM who I AM," or in some translations, "I AM what I AM." Also, "I AM has sent me," or "The Lord, the God of your fathers . . . has sent me to you." (These come from various Bibles.)

Remember Moses had been in isolation, tending the flocks of his father-in-law and had had much silence and time for meditation and prayer. He was well versed in Egyptian religion but was not prepared for this experience. We know that he followed the Lord God after that. He followed the "I AM," his Inner Knowing.

To describe the Indescribable posed a problem for the writer of Exodus. But the attempt has opened up Judaism and Christianity as well as Islam, to a multitude of definitions. I do not suggest that this

Treatise is the last word about *The Word*, but I would like to propose that for us of the Aquarian Age there is yet another meaning.

A question: Could I AM be referring to the Kundalini Energy, the Fire Energy, the Christ, the Holy Spirit that we are focusing this writing on? Could we find in the I AM statements of Jesus a clue to this idea? John Shelby Spong proposes that. He says that the translators of John would often add a subject to I AM even when there was no subject in the Greek (page 204f).

The example he gives is from John 8:28, when Jesus says: "When you have lifted up the Son of man then you will know that I am he." He says that the Greek for this is "When you have lifted up the Son of man then you will know I AM."

He further writes that when one knows I AM one will see the glorified Christ. This does not refer, he says, to lifting up the Son of man on the cross, but the lifting of the Son of man in our consciousness. Then we will experience glory, exaltation, ascension. All of these describe the result of raising the Kundalini Energy to the seventh Chakra. Then we experience the glory of God, the I AM. The Son of man, in my teaching, is our Inner Spirit. When it is lifted up the Glory is experienced.

In John 8:58 Jesus said, "Truly, truly, I say to you, before Abraham was, I AM." Interesting that the verbs are mixed: "Was," past tense and "AM," present. That is an indication that I AM was considered a noun by the translators, not a pronoun (I) and a verb (AM). It is the *Word*.

I AM was in the beginning. I AM is in the present. I AM, a statement of Being, is who you and I are, and as we become conscious of this we will be Glorified.

When we use the Word, "I AM," we are declaring God and it is when the object of that "Being" verb is negative that trials and tribulations come to us. We do not realize the strength of that Holy Spirit that is the foundation of our body, our mind, our feelings and within our Soul trying to find Its way to Ascension.

Corinne Heline in Volume I of her NEW AGE BIBLE INTERPRETATION (page 232) points out that the Third Commandment decrees that we must not take the name of the Lord God in vain. Thus, if we think or speak the negative with I AM we would be desecrating the Name. Jesus said in Matthew 12:31, 32, that a sin against the Holy Spirit was unforgivable. Do these two go together? Her/His name is the name I AM, that Living Spirit within you and me.

39

Emma Curtis Hopkins calls the I AM, the God within us. She says I AM is the central flame common to but hidden deep in all mankind. She says, "Some people have called that conquering central flame, which can so overpower all human sensation and mental awareness, the I AM of man, the Spirit of man, the Spirit of God." (HIGH MYSTICISM, page 234)

Matthew Fox in THE COMING OF THE COSMIC CHRIST says that the Cosmic Christ is the I AM in every creature (page 154). Also that I AM is an expression of the DIVINE ONE.

Charles Fillmore, co-founder of Unity, says that the Son of man is the real I AM in each individual. "I AM is Christ," he wrote.

Carl Jung in SYMBOLS OF TRANSFORMATION says that Christ is the Self, is the archetype of the Spirit.

Christ identified himself with the serpent (John 3:14) and said that the Son of man must be lifted up to eternal life just as Moses lifted up the serpent in the wilderness. This applies to our subject if we accept that our Christ is our I AM. The cross for us is our physical living experiences and we are lifted up by our Inner Christ, the I AM.

From this suggestion, i.e. that Jesus' words on the I AM refer to that Kundalini Energy, that Holy Spirit, let us seek Truth from some of his statements. I shall quote them from this viewpoint adding "is" as a verb and using I AM as the subject.

John 6:48: I AM (is) the bread of life.

8:12: I AM (is) the light of the world; he who follows me will not walk in darkness but will have the light of life.

8:23: I AM (is) from above; you are of this world
I AM (is) not of this world.

10:11: I AM (is) the good shepherd.

10:36: I AM (is) the Son of God.

14:6: I AM (is) the way and the truth and the life; no one comes to the Father (I AM) but by me (Christ).

This last quoted verse is very important to our Thesis. "I AM the way." The Way is infinite just as the Kundalini, the Holy Spirit is infinite. And Truth?

Humankind has been trying to define It forever, but Truth cannot be defined. It is like the Way. Truth, Life, the Way result from the I AM. They are the I AM, the spirit, the Invincible One beyond description or interpretation or definition, but each of us

KNOWS, for we experience all of them. They are the trinity of our Soul, of our I AM. That Soul is impregnated with a Spark of All That Is. That Spark is the I AM. That Spark is Divine Energy.

In some of these verses I have replaced Father with I AM, for That is what Jesus was referring to. In that time the patriarchal God was honored by being called Him, Father. Jesus gave all credit to his Father, his I AM. He never took credit to his small self. The Father (I AM) was his Teacher, his Guide and was within him and he was within the I AM. (John 17:21)

All of these are quite intelligible when we accept that the I AM is that Holy Spirit within you and me. That Divine Energy is bread (Holy Spirit); light (Sun); door (entrance into a spiritual realm); good shepherd (caring for souls); the life of the physical and the resurrection from physical attachment.

In Isaiah 43:10,11, we have reference to I AM. The Lord was speaking. Verse 10: ". . . I AM He." And Verse 11: "I AM the Lord, and besides me there is no savior."

Compare this with Jesus' statement recorded in John 8:28:

> When you have lifted up the Son of man, then you will know that I AM he, and I do nothing on my own authority but speak thus as the Father (I AM) taught me.

This verse says it all: Our I AM is the Lord. The I AM is our life, and our Truth. To Be is I AM. We have no life without I AM. I AM is our Way, our Path, our Journey.

For centuries there have been those looking for the "Lost Word." Could I AM be that Lost Word?

Thomas Troward, who wrote many books from the metaphysical/mystical point of view, thought so. He lived in India for many years and thus his writings reflected Hindu teaching. Consider some of what he has written on the Lost Word:

> "The 'Lost Word' which we have been seeking to discover with pain, and cost, and infinite study, has been all the time in our heart and in our mouth—it is nothing else than that familiar expression which we use so many times a day—I AM. This is the Divine Name revealed to Moses at the burning bush, and is the Word that is enshrined in the name Jehovah . . . "
>
> (BIBLE MYSTERY AND BIBLE MEANING, page 159).

Claim for yourself all that Is. Yours is Life and that is *To Be. Am, is, are, was, were* become the same as I AM when we consciously accept It. The I Am rises up to the Untimate Being and we are One. That Energy rises up our spine, opens our intellect, feeling nature, etheric chakras, and we are finally at One with I Am, consciously. We each are recipients of the Bread of life and we become that Bread, as did Jesus Christ and we go forth to feed the multitude.

Let us look now briefly, very briefly, at the phrase "Bread of Life" as relating to I AM, the Spirit Within. In a number of verses recorded that Jesus spoke, he referred to Bread, to the Bread of Life. In John 6:48-51 he said, "I AM the bread of life, living bread which came down from heaven." He further said that if anyone eat of this bread, he will live forever: "and the bread which I shall give for the life of the world is my flesh."

Is this Bread not the I AM, the food, the Energy, the Spirit? It IS and I AM. I AM—God is I AM, the Bread from heaven. According to CRUDEN'S COMPLETE CONCORDANCE, bread when used figuratively is the bread of life and is the Christ. The Christ is the I AM and the Holy Spirit.

God is I AM, personally and spiritually. Total consciousness of that I AM, that dwells within, is our Goal.

Chapter IX

LOAVES AND FISHES AND BREAD OF LIFE

John 6:1-15, 22-69

In John 5 it is recorded that Jesus gave a long discourse to the Jews who had criticized him for healing on the Sabbath and telling the man who was healed to take up his bed or pallet and walk. It was against the Law to carry a pallet on the Sabbath. According to this scripture the Jews sought to kill Jesus because he broke the Laws of the Sabbath and called God his own Father, making himself equal with God. (Verse 18)

The sermon which followed their criticism reiterated over and over the Son's activity due to the will of God. Let us go now to John 6.

After his long discourse, Jesus went to the other side of the Sea of Galilee/Tiberias to have some quiet, but a multitude followed him because they had seen his healing of diseases. He went up on a mountain and sat down with his disciples. The large crowd was composed of many going to Jerusalem for the Jewish Passover. It was a great opportunity for him to teach a large number of pilgrims from all over the area, and he chose to teach that which would fill their hearts and minds and not their bellies.

This feeding of the 5000 has been taken literally by most of Christendom. It is considered one of Jesus' greatest miracles, and indeed it was. I am not going to try to change anyone's mind on that score, but I should like you to consider an alternative interpretation, as I feel this myth has a great teaching for us and illustrates the power of the Divine Energy that Jesus expressed in his Journey on the earth plane.

43

Jesus saw the hunger for Truth in the eyes of the multitude. He turned to Philip, an apostle, and asked him how they were going to buy bread to feed the multitude. "This he said to test him, for he himself knew what he would do." (Verse 6)

Philip symbolizes power, according to Fillmore's teaching on the TWELVE POWERS OF MAN. Power can come from thoughts or Spirit. Philip answered from thought. He pointed out that 200 days labor (200 denarii) would not buy enough bread for them—it was an impossible task according to the power of the intellect. After all, there were 5000 men plus the women and children. Jesus had posed a test and Philip failed it.

Andrew (strength, a strong man) told Jesus that a lad had five barley loaves and two fish, but he couldn't see how that would feed the multitude. Then Jesus told the disciples to "make the people sit down." He had them sit in groups of fifty and a hundred, according to Mark 6:40.

He took the loaves and fish and did the most important thing. He gave thanks.

Giving thanks to their god has been the way of humankind forever. Various religious rituals in memory of their god was not very different than the ritual of the use of bread and wine that was substituted for the flesh and blood of other gods, such as Osiris, Adonis, Dionysus.

These rituals all contained the giving of thanks to the Creator for sustenance not only for one's physical but for spiritual needs. We have always known that all comes from the All; either consciously or subconsciously we have known this.

In John 6:11 it is recorded that Jesus distributed the fish and bread to those who were seated, and when they had eaten their fill, Jesus told his disciples to gather up what was left over and they gathered enough bread to fill twelve baskets.

"When the people saw the sign which he had done, they said, 'This is indeed the prophet who is come into the world.'" (Verse 14) A prophet is one who receives inspiration from the Spirit.

When we look at this myth literally we are astounded in considering how many were fed in a short time—5000 men plus women and children! This scripture says Jesus himself distributed the bread and fish. (John 6:11) Matthew 14:15 records that it was evening when the needs of the people were brought to Jesus' attention. To feed 5000+ people bread and fish would have taken them far into the night. And consider the uproar that would have occurred if they had seen Jesus manifest food out of thin air. Would they have remained seated? How would the children have reacted? No, this interpretation just does not fit our intellectual analysis of the miracle. But then, miracles are not meant to be analyzed, are they? However, there is a spiritual interpretation of the miracle that I should like to present.

Although I have not witnessed it, I think that one who is of high enough spiritual consciousness can manifest articles out of the atoms of the air which are invisible to us. Corinne Heline in Volume V of her series, page 95, says that the highly evolved one can control the atoms and multiply them into an object. However, she says, the active one must have a nucleus upon which to operate, which Jesus did in the five loaves and two fish. She says imaging, the power of faith, and understanding the Creative Mind Power are necessary.

We know people who have been at the ashram of Sri Satya Sai Baba and have witnessed his producing objects. (See GOD HAS GIVEN US EVERY GOOD THING, by Roy Eugene Davis.) They testify that it is possible.

However, I feel the evidence from the scriptural account suggests that this food was from the spiritual, from the Kundalini Energy source. This was the Bread of Life that Jesus gave them.

In a discussion of the *manna* in the desert that the Israelites were sustained by, I suggest that the *manna* was the Kundalini Energy in each one that flowed and fed them physically and spiritually. They were sustained for forty years (the time it takes for completion of a task) by the "bread from heaven."

In John 6:32, 33 Jesus refers to that account and he says Moses did not give the Israelites the bread from heaven, but "my Father gives you the true bread from heaven. For the bread of God is that which comes down from heaven and gives life to the world." This was spoken soon after he had fed the 5000. The bread that had satisfied their hunger was the bread of God, not physical barley bread—it was the Bread of Life.

Bread symbolizes spiritual nourishment. Fish symbolize the Christ. Remember the symbol for Christianity was the fish, and was the symbol for Jesus the Christ. So we have the Christ (the Inner Spirit) and bread (spiritual nourishment) together fulfilling the needs of the people, both physical and spiritual. It is the Christ which is within and comes from heaven, from God. It is this food that gave them the strength to go on about their daily living.

We have in the feeding of the 5000 Jesus the Christ passing on to others the experience of that great Divine Energy. It fulfilled their needs physically, emotionally and spiritually. This is baptism by the Spirit. He, like the guru, had only to look deeply into expectant eyes and the Energy from his eyes would move the Kundalini Energy in the recipient. He could do this quickly, for it only takes a glance to arouse this Energy. Touching and chanting will do the same.

Jesus was on a high mountain symbolizing high consciousness. The thoughts of the people were open, and his gestures, his looking, his attention changed them and they felt fulfilled.

Now let us apply this to us personally. The 5000 symbolizes the thoughts from our intellect which is always vacant, hungry and empty until it receives spiritual nourishment. It is our Christ that brings spiritual nourishment to our thoughts. Until we are aware of that, we will struggle with earth living; we will be hungry. Turning to that Holy Spirit is our Task and our Glory.

The seven chakra centers when blessed by the Christ become full and overflowing and the body and consciousness is filled. This will give us Enlightenment. This is our aim. Until then our disciples are still learning and depending on the intellect to fulfill our needs. The Christ Spirit, the Holy Spirit, takes care of those needs.

Jesus-Sophia fed the thousands of hungry people who were looking for surcease from hunger. Although the majority were masculine, the feminine also is hungry as are the offspring of the masculine and feminine. It is the same with us, for we often overlook our spiritual needs by filling our physical needs. Then we become confused believing that being filled physically will satisfy us. But our spiritual needs are unfulfilled. The 5000+ of the multitude were not satisfied either as later they went looking for Jesus. (John 6:22f) Our 5000 thoughts are restless also until we find our own Inner Christ.

Jesus fed the hungry, which is a mothering role. Thus his Sophia came forth in his spiritual baptism of each one. How this myth has inspired millions and most have believed that only Jesus could perform this miracle, but it is in the capability of all of us when Centered in our Christ.

We understand that our Inner Christ and our spiritual knowledge is waiting to fulfill our needs and the needs of others. Our feminine Divine Energy fills our every longing and we serve others with it.

My Inner Soul, my Holy Spirit, found the 5000 masculine thoughts satisfied me for a period of time, but ultimately I hungered again. I know that my Spirit now feeds the 5000 thoughts and there will be plenty left over for the Infinite is continuous and is never used up. There is always more. When I have been Enlightened by the filling of my thoughts with the I AM Knowing, I need quiet and rest in order to "lave" in the Delightful feelings that fill my Soul, my mind and my body. So I go apart awhile and sing my Song to my Self, to my Soul.

Thus did Jesus-Sophia. He/she went away to the mountain because the people's hunger was satisfied and they wanted to make him a king. (John 6:15) But he had no egoistic desires. They did not understand that his mission was to do the Will of his Father, which was a demonstration of the love and spiritual upliftment by the Spirit, the Bread of Life. Jesus-Sophia knew the Mission and it was not to gain honors on the physical plane. He/she was on the spiritual plane. His feminine Spirit, Sophia or Wisdom, had done Her work and he withdrew from the crowd and his disciples in peace.

Jesus was very uplifted after his feeding of the 5000. There is no Energy loss when the guru baptizes others with this Holy Energy. Neither is there any Energy loss when we feed our own thoughts or feed others. The Divine Energy, the Holy Spirit, fills us with Ecstasy and Joy. We give thanks to start It to flowing and we give thanks for the result.

Jesus Teaches on the Bread of Life

I shall now skip to John 6:22-69 to discuss the next encounter Jesus had with the multitude and his teaching on the Bread of Life.

The people went searching for Jesus after he had fed them. They decided that he had gone to Capernaum. They loaded into boats (thoughts that carry us across the unconscious) and went across the Sea of Tiberias (spiritual insight) to Capernaum. They were seeking the prophet who had fed them. Capernaum symbolizes comfort, compassion. When we are confused we seek a place of comfort, of understanding, and we find the Christ in that state of Being. When once we are fed by the Bread of Life, we may not understand this experience and we seek more.

Jesus was in Capernaum. He had walked across the sea without fear and had performed another miracle. (John 6:16-21) When the people found him they asked how he had gotten there. His reply was that they were seeking him so that they could have more loaves. Esoterically he meant the Bread of Life. He said to them that they should not labor for food which perishes, but for food

47

(Holy Spirit) which endures to Eternal Life, which he said the Son of man would give, for God had set his seal on the Son. (Verse 27)

This verse directly supports my interpretation. The Son is the Spirit, a Spark of God, which when sought and given attention will give us Eternal Life, the Kingdom of Heaven. That is what our Search is about. The Bread from Heaven gives us life but we take many side roads to recognize It.

Then the people asked what they should do "to be doing the works of God." Jesus-Sophia gave a short pithy answer which carries deep teaching.

> This is the work of God, that you believe in him whom he has sent.
> (Verse 29)

The One, God had sent, was the Son, not Jesus the Son of man, but the Son that abides in each man, woman and child, the Holy Spirit.

They did not understand. They were literalists. They thought that he, Jesus, was the Son just as many have believed through the ages, never realizing that the Son is the Spirit in each one of us. Our Divine Spirit is the Son. They reminded him that their fathers had been provided *manna* in the desert and in effect said, "Show us such a sign."

He answered that it was not Moses who provided the Bread from Heaven but the Father that gives the true bread from heaven and that the Bread of God comes down from heaven and gives life to the world.

Coming down from heaven refers to the Spirit of the High All-ness that lies dormant in our body and consciousness until we awaken to this Bread that feeds us life. That life is in all on this earth plane. That life is the breath of the animals, the energy of the Sun on growing foliage, the life of Mother Earth and Father Sky. All comes from the Bread from Heaven.

This Allness abides in our consciousness as the Kundalini Energy which is, of course, the bread.

The people asked Jesus for this bread and he proceeded to give a sermon on the Bread of Life. He said, "I AM, the bread of life. . . ." (Verse 35) Or, as we have suggested, "I AM (is) the Bread of Life." Our Christ is the Bread of Life. When we consciously come to the I AM we shall not hunger for physical or spiritual food, nor shall we thirst.

48

The people did not understand. They thought he was talking about himself personally as the Bread of Life. They pointed out that they knew his physical parents and where he was born, so how could he have come down from heaven?

He says again: "I AM, the bread of life." (Verse 48)

He pointed out that their fathers ate the *manna* and died. Then he defined the Bread of Heaven again. He said that the Bread from Heaven when eaten would give life and eternal life.

He was defining God, the I AM, as the Bread of Heaven.

> "I AM (is) the living bread which came down from heaven. . . ."
> (Verse 51)

His Christ, the I AM, was speaking through him. The I AM, as we have explained before, is that living Presence which is within us, within our psyche, our conscious and unconscious awareness.

> Truly, truly, I say to you, unless you eat the flesh of the Son of man and drink his blood you have no life in you. (Verse 53)

Verse 53 is difficult for us to understand, for we have been conditioned to believe that Jesus gave his flesh and blood so that we might have Eternal Life. It is not my task to refute this with theological argument. However, consider this: If the Son of man is the Holy Spirit then our very flesh and blood is of the Son, for there is no life in the flesh, in the blood, without the Spirit. The blood is the carrier of that Spirit. Therefore it is our Son that gives us life.

Also, a literal translation of this scripture, assuming that the Christ in Jesus was referring to himself as the Son of man, would lead us to believe that if the Christ (Son) had not come in the human fleshly body of Jesus we would not have his great teaching that has evolved the Western world to a higher level of awareness of Inner Divinity.

I should add that many Bible scholars believe that this verse was added by Church authorities to command church members to take the communion service, the Eucharist, as necessary for their life.

Of course, the listeners did not understand. Even his disciples did not, and some left him. He tried to explain what he meant:

> It is the spirit that gives life, the flesh is of no avail; the words that I have spoken to you are spirit and life. (Verse 63)

It takes one who is advanced to a Mystical level to understand these words.

Consider this interpretation: It is the Spirit of Christ that gives life, not his flesh and blood. He meant, "Listen with your inner ear to what your Spirit interprets my words to mean. It is the effervescent Spirit and life of the Spirit that I have been speaking about."

Many disciples left, but the apostles (our human faculties turned toward our Christ but not complete) stayed. He asked them if they also wanted to leave him. The stalwart Peter, who understood more deeply than the others, asked where they would go since they believed that he was the Holy One of God. At that moment Peter believed, but later he had his doubts about following the Savior. The apostles did not seem to believe completely until they experienced the Holy Spirit at Pentecost. Then they fully understood Jesus' teaching.

Our thoughts control us, raise doubts, have limited understanding of what our intuition, an undefinable word, tells us. It is so far ahead of our logical, reasoning thoughts that we often miss the meaning and sometimes turn away in fear. But our apostles (thoughts) stay with the Spirit and eventually are filled and are ENLIGHTENED—filled with Light. This intuition is the Bread of Heaven. That is the Holy One of God, that Christ. Our body carries that Christ across the sea of Galilee to Capernaum. We find there the compassion and concern from our Inner Spirit. Our thoughts still have doubts and often turn away, back to the mundane world and thus we may lose the chance to inherit Eternal Life.

Each one of us is body, mind, spirit, and heart. The physical, intellectual, spiritual and feeling nature are our heritage. When we listen and believe our Holy Spirit teachings, all will become unified.

The Christ taught beyond our understanding, but when we advance on our spiritual path we will understand and Know that "I AM WHO I AM" expresses our Oneness and our recognition comes through our Christ speaking from within. Listen! Do not turn away.

We hunger for Loaves and Fishes. We hunger for the Bread of Life. All are from the Christ, the Holy Spirit within, and we are fed by the Divine Energy, Sophia.

Perhaps I should remind the reader that when I speak of the Holy Spirit I am using accepted Christian language for that Kundalini Energy, that feminine Energy which was named Sophia by the Gnostics. Since I am writing for Christians I use the traditional *Holy Spirit* as designating that *Inner Fire* called the Kundalini by Hindus.

Chapter X

I AM, THE GOOD SHEPHERD

John 10

Jesus spent many hours, many words, much energy teaching the Jews who lived in Israel. He also taught the Samaritans and the Gentiles. But it was to the Tribes of Israel that he was sent. He did not discount the teachings of Moses, of the Torah, the teaching of the Jews. What he did was to let go of those Laws that were keeping the people from evolving spiritually. The *status quo* could not tolerate this teaching and thus was always trying to entangle him in their rational Jewish Law. He taught that a person must go beyond that accepted teaching of the organized religion and move to an awareness of the Father within as the Holy Spirit. He taught Love as opposed to Law, although he said he came to fulfill the Law. That Law, above all others, is to love God, neighbor and your Self completely.

This also fits our modern age. The Christian church dogma is embedded in the unconscious of the members or former members. The literal interpretation has been a Light for millions of souls which have come and gone and have come again. However, many are realizing that Jesus' teaching carries a symbolic meaning for them. The evolution of many in the realization of WHO they are is gaining momentum. This evolution of spiritual consciousness cannot be stopped. Many are ready.

The teaching of Jesus gives us insight into our own personal spiritual Journey centered in the Holy Spirit.

As an introduction to John 10, I should like to suggest that all individuals, consciously or unconsciously, are on a Journey back to the Source of Light. This Journey has been explained by many religions. There are many commonalities in all of these teachings and these are recognized when one interprets the scriptures symbolically. There is a level of teaching for each soul.

There are at least Three broad Levels of Spirit consciousness with many sublevels. These Three Levels are the Mental, the Mystical, and the Absolute. These need a short explanation. Many of us go through each level in this lifetime. Many of us cling to one level or the other because we are not ready to move on. We are where we are meant to be.

On the Mental Level the individual is at the conscious level of Believing, of Faith, of receiving Truth. Their thoughts are centered on a belief in the teaching of the Founder of their religion. This belief causes them to read and understand the Scripture on a literal level. They follow the teachings of the church or temple and the authorities without question. They affirm through thought control that all Good will come to them. When at this level they are fulfilling the Law and are satisfied. Seekers at this level make up the large majority of humankind who are religious, both in the West and in the East.

There are many, however, that are not satisfied spiritually at this level. They have a dis–ease. Something more is calling them. They search and sometimes find the answer. These may be destined for the Mystical Level in this life or another. The Mystic turns from the outer to the Inner to find their Holy Spirit (known by other names in other religions). They turn from the world and center their thoughts, desires, actions, Beingness on the Guidance from that Holy Spirit. It may bring them all forms of joy, ecstasy and bliss. They let go of attachments to centeredness in thought and turn to the Spirit to guide their thoughts. They are devoted to *Experiencing* the Truth. They have gone beyond Believing. They KNOW. (See my book FROM METAPHYSICAL TO MYSTICAL.)

The third level is impossible to describe adequately in words, for few of us have experienced this level and do not have words to explain it. It is believed that there have been gurus, avatars, founders of various religions who have achieved this level, Jesus the Christ being our greatest demonstrator. These are great Teachers who are One with All That Is; One with Truth, One with the Beloved, and have incarnated in order to teach humankind how to reach that Oneness. When Jesus said, "I and the Father are one," (John 10:30) he was stoned by the Jews. This statement indicates Being in the Absolute. This is Being the Absolute. (See Emma Curtis Hopkins' HIGH MYSTICISM for more description of the Absolute level).

Now many Searchers have the experience of Being the Absolute, but it is a brief experience of total Oneness felt as Bliss, Ecstasy— "out of this world." This calls the person on. Always being at that level of Awareness is the Goal.

With this background let us now turn to John 10 where these different levels are exemplified.

The Parable of the Sheep, the Sheepfold, the robber, the Shepherd, the Door, the gatekeeper told by Jesus brings us back to our Thesis and especially as we hear Jesus using the Word, I AM.

The Parable was spoken after Jesus had healed a man who had been blind from birth. In answer to the question "Are we also blind?" from the Pharisees, Jesus answered (Verses 1-5):

> Truly, truly, I say to you, he who does not enter the sheepfold by the door but climbs in by another way, that man is a thief and a robber; but he who enters by the door is the shepherd of the sheep. To him the gatekeeper opens; the sheep hear his voice, and he calls his own sheep by name and leads them out. When he has brought out all his own, he goes before them, and the sheep follow him, for they know his voice. A stranger they will not follow, but they will flee from him, for they do not know the voice of strangers.

Jesus explanation of this Parable is found in Verses 7-18 and 25-30. I shall not quote them; you might like to read them.

First I should like to identify what I believe the terms listed symbolize:

Sheepfold—Kingdom of Heaven, the Ecstatic state of Allness

Sheep—our thoughts which are docile, gentle, easily led, followers of the Holy Spirit

Shepherd—the I AM, the Holy Spirit, the Kundalini, the Christ

Door—opening our consciousness to the Holy Spirit, entrance into the Kingdom of Heaven

Gatekeeper—the Godhead

Pharisees and Jews—negative thoughts which deny the Shepherd's guidance.

There are a number of I AM statements which the Christ used as She spoke through Jesus. She said:

"I AM, the door of the sheep." (Verse 7)

"I AM, the door, if anyone enters by me, he will be saved and will go in and out and find pasture." (Verse 9)

"I AM, the good shepherd."   (Verse 11, 14)

"I AM, the Son of God."   (Verse 36)

"I AM, in the Father."   (Verse 38)

It was not the human Jesus saying these words but the I AM, Sophia, the Holy Spirit of Jesus speaking through him.

With this background I shall briefly give my explanation of the parable.

In Verse 1 Jesus said that one must enter the sheepfold (Kingdom of Heaven) through the door of the Sheepfold and cannot enter another way. That person would be a thief and a robber. The opening of the door to the Kingdom of Heaven is our conscious move toward that level; it is opening our consciousness to Truth. We are thieves or robbers when we try to enter the Kingdom without turning to the Holy Spirit (the Shepherd) to protect us, to guide our life and thoughts. The thief or robber could also be our allegiance to a religious teaching that is not leading us toward the Kingdom.

Verse 2 says that he who enters by the door is the shepherd of the sheep. This door gives us a conscious awareness of the Shepherd, the Christ within, which will lead our sheep, our gentle thoughts, into the sheepfold, the Kingdom.

The gatekeeper is All That Is, the Godhead. God knows the need to call the sheep, our thoughts, to the safety of the Shepherd. The Gatekeeper, the Godhead, is our own Holy Spirit finally come Home and will take our thoughts, lead our thoughts. (Verse 4)

When our Law-filled thoughts let go of the belief that they alone can lead us to the sheepfold, and become gentle and pliant, then we will follow the Good Shepherd, the Christ.

A stranger may try to lead our thoughts (Verse 5). This stranger is the world. We are so immersed in the world through our family, our government, our friends, our work, our religion, that we can ignore our Inner Spirit and miss the Kingdom. But Jesus said that once our thoughts have become aware of our Spirit Guidance we will follow the world no more. Following the Spirit will be primary. The robbers and thieves will not enter our pristine Kingdom or prevent us from entering It.

Jesus the Christ was speaking this at first to the Pharisees. Pharisees symbolize authoritarian thoughts that arise from the unconscious that bind one to external forms of religion and to the external world (man).

54

Thoughts in our unconscious, gained from our permeable childhood and early adulthood, can prevent us from changing our spiritual allegiance. The religion we are born into has first call on our spiritual awareness. It is sometimes most difficult to let those thoughts go and find our Peace in another frame of reference.

Also, other thoughts in our unconscious can be our greatest block to follow our Inner Guide, the Good Shepherd. These are memories from our mundane experiences. Most of us do not come to the level of searching for Who we are until we are about 30 or 40 years old or older. Many negative experiences and thoughts have been stuffed into our unconscious by this time. These must be cleansed—looked at, admitted, loved and forgiven—before we can move forward on our Journey. Carl Jung's teaching specifies dream interpretation as a way of clearing the negative from our unconscious as well as meditation and active imagination (having a conversation with our Inner Self). Other psychologies stress therapy, talking out and experiencing. Until these are cleared, until our Shadow and our Complexes are recognized, we cannot have a happy whole life. Clearing the unconscious allows unity with the conscious mind and the superconscious, the I AM. Until then our Pharisaic thoughts will block our progress.

Jesus the Christ then tries to interpret the parable for the crowd. The listeners are called Jews. (Verse 19) They suggested that Jesus had a demon, was mad and should not be listened to. These symbolize thoughts that are negative to any new teaching. They are not docile thoughts but thoughts based on one's past traditional religious teaching.

Again, we must remember that the recorder of the Book of John spoke in symbolic, esoteric terms much of the time. It cannot be read literally and understood from a spiritual stance. It is the most mystical of all the Gospels.

Jesus identified the Spirit, the I AM, not Jesus the man, as the door to the Kingdom of Heaven. The Spirit, the Shepherd opens the door but unless we turn to that door, face it, knock on it, it will not open. The Christ Spirit gives life to all on this planet. This Christ leads us as a Good Shepherd. We cannot get lost when we turn within for our Way. The Gatekeeper recognizes our Christ, our Holy Spirit, and opens the Way.

The Grace of the Good Shepherd, the All in All which is the Christ, will lead us. This Good Shepherd hears our cries of pain and longing. This Good Shepherd, through Grace, will open the door to the Sheepfold, the Kingdom.

Jesus the Christ said there were other sheep who would heed his voice and then "shall be one flock, one shepherd." (Verse 16)

This is the Ultimate that Jesus so often spoke of. His belief that all would be One.

The Christ said that the "Father loves me, because I lay down my life, that I may take it again." (Verse 17)

When we are born into the physical realm, when our Holy Spirit is entrapped in a physical body, we lay down our life, but we take it again when we are "born anew" and realize Who we really are. The Christ dies in our corporeal consciousness but lives again in incorporeal thoughts and feelings. We have the power to lay it down, to be born from physical parents which we choose, but we have the power to take it up to the Heights of Spiritual Oneness.

The life and teachings of Jesus is the Christian's criteria for advancement to the Kingdom. His teaching was too deep for the followers of 2000 years ago, and is not understood by many people today. St. Paul's teaching has been *writ larg* for most of organized Christian teachings. However, much of St. Paul's mystical teaching has also been ignored.

Jesus taught that it was the Higher Being, Searcher of Hearts, Supreme One that he was following. He tells us:

> But my sheep hear my voice, and I know them, and they follow me and I give them eternal life . . .　　　　　(Verse 27, 28a)

He gives all credit to that Greatest of All, his Father. He says that his Father gave these sheep to him. (Verse 29)

Our Christ, our Holy Spirit, our Divine Energy is Guided by the Godhead. Our God is our Inspirer. Our God is our Holy Spirit. Our God is That Which I AM. And that *I AM who I AM* is Truth for those who are at the mystic level.

And then the Christ declared:

> "I and the Father are one."　　　　　(Verse 30)

That is the Absolute stage of our Journey. Our Christ is not separate in our consciousness. We recognize that our Christ and the God of All are One. That is the Kingdom of Heaven, that is Nirvana, that is Satori, that is Enlightenment. When we reach that High Estate we are above every thought, every personal desire. Our thoughts are One with our Christ, our Intuition. Our masculine and feminine, thoughts and intuition, are One.

We all have flashes of this State of Being. Our greatest creative acts come when we are fully One with the God of All. It is through the non-thought that the great Thoughts come. This is an experience of being in the Kingdom of Heaven consciousness. Jesus the Christ taught that it is within us. (Luke 17:21) Then we are in the Sheepfold and are One with the Godhead. Our Holy Spirit has found her way back to the Kingdom.

This is all explained through the teaching on the Kundalini Energy. That is our Life. The Good Shepherd carries the Shepherd's Staff and uses it to bring the sheep, the conscious thoughts, into Oneness. Thus our consciousness of Who we are is complete. That Staff, the spine, is the conveyer of this high Energy to the top of the head, the top of the brain, where abides All That Is, our only One that is All, I AM.

Thus we have the people (thoughts on the Mental Level), advancing to turning to the Inner Christ for life (the Mystic Level) and then being at One with the Father (the Absolute Level, who is ALL KNOWING, ONE I AM. We know our Path. We know on which level we abide. We know that our spiritual evolution is inevitable.

· Wisdom-Sophia has spoken!

The Jews were ready to stone Jesus after his explanation of the Sheep and the Shepherd and after he said, "I and the Father are one." His response to them is given in Verses 34-36:

> Is it not written in your law, "I said, you are gods"? If he called them gods to whom the word of God comes (and scripture cannot be broken) do you say of him whom the Father consecrated and sent into the world, "You are blaspheming" because I said "I am the Son of God"?

Jesus tried to quiet them by pointing out that their law acclaimed each one as god. This refers to Psalm 82:6.

How do you respond to this statement "You are gods"? Do you believe that? Does it have a ring of Truth for you? Or do you want to pass that by with "It is a mistranslation"?

Now remember, Jesus did not say "You are God" for this would be untrue at their consciousness level. Only the Christ, the Holy Spirit, can claim that. The Christ through Jesus said "I AM, the Son of God." In other words the I AM is the Son of God. Nowhere else in scripture does Jesus, in referring to himself, use these words "Son of God." Many others used this term when referring to him. This title "Son of God" was one that his followers bestowed upon him, but he did say, "I and the Father are one." He also said, "the Father is in me and I AM in the Father." (Verse 38)

So what does this teaching mean for us?

To be designated as a god indicates our sublime consciousness based only on the Spirit within. To try to understand this logically is impossible, but to understand it intuitively is possible.

We are the manifestation of Spirit come to earth, living in a physical body and ego state of consciousness. None of this is separate from God, all of it is God. We are That, but our awareness of it is crippled by our physical experience and so our Journey is to know our SOURCE, our I AM, through experiencing That Which Is. When we have reached that Feeling Awareness, not thought awareness, we are complete in God. Our potential is to be conscious of "Ye are gods." When the Christ reiterates time after time: "I and the Father are one," he is not bragging but stating a Truth at that instant of consciousness. What was so great about Jesus was that he was aware of the Truth continuously and spoke and acted from that Center. He did not place himself over the populace, over us as Seekers on the Path. What he said was, "You are gods, but do not recognize it. I realize my Oneness. I am teaching you how to realize the potential that lies within your consciousness. In Truth you are the Son of God. Realize this and Be It."

"You are gods." Can you accept that?

The listeners were not convinced. Neither are most human beings today. To realize our deep I AM fully makes us One. "I AM, the Son of God" is Truth. Not the human as the Son of God, but the Christ, I AM, the Son/Daughter of God.

They tried to arrest Jesus but he escaped. He left that area and went to the Jordan River where John the Baptist had baptized him. There he had reassurance as to his Mission as he remembered the Voice from Heaven saying to him, "This is my beloved Son with whom I am well pleased." (Matthew 3:17)

There he was restored and many came to him and believed in him.

Thus ends Chapter X. And the "Glory of the Lord shone 'round about him." Amen

Chapter XI

THE SON FROM THE FATHER

John 5:19-47

In Chapter VI, I have gone into some detail on the meaning of the phrases Son of man. I should like to enlarge upon that teaching in this Chapter for in these verses Jesus refers to the Son, Son of man, and Son of God.

We have here a long discourse from Jesus Christ in which he/she focuses on the Son and the Father. "Son" is mentioned ten times; Father is mentioned twelve times. It is a most important teaching on the relationship of the Son and the Father. Son of man is used once; Son of God once also. Son is used more often.

I should like you to consider now the relationship between the words *Sun* and *Son*. I believe this is important if I am to support my Thesis that Son is the feminine Spirit, the Holy Spirit which is the Life Force, the Kundalini. The Father is that Godhead with whom the Christ of Jesus was One. His Holy Spirit was One with the Absolute. Son of man is the Christ in the human consciousness; Son of God is the Christ in the enlightened state.

Son and the Sun have often been compared, for the Son, the Divine Energy, is the Light of the Soul, while the Sun is the Light of all life. So let us see what Sun symbolizes, which may enlighten us as to the Son that Jesus spoke of so often in this chapter.

Cirlót says in referring to sun symbolism:

> Another alchemic concept, that of the *Sol in homine* (of the invisible essence of the celestial Sun which nourishes the inborn fire of Man), is an early pointer to the way the astral body has lately been interpreted by psychoanalysts, narrowing its meaning down to that of heat or energy, equivalent to the fire of life and the libido. Hence, Jung's point that the Sun is, in truth, a symbol of the source of life and of the ultimate wholeness of man.   (A DICTIONARY OF SYMBOLS, page 319)

From Jung:

> The psychic life-force, the libido, symbolizes itself in the sun, or personifies itself in figures of heroes with solar attributes.
>
> (SYMBOLS OF TRANSFORMATION, page 202)

This libido is used for creativity, or for begetting offspring, or for work, or for sexual pleasure, or for raising one's consciousness to Oneness. So we can see that Sun and Son with the same pronunciation is that libido. It has sun-like attributes. This Son or Sun is within each one of us.

From The Nag Hammadi Library:

> Now Son of Man harmonized with Sophia, his consort, and revealed a great androgynous light. Some call this masculine name "Savior, Begetter of All things." His feminine name is called "Sophia, All-Begettress." Some call her "Pistis."
>
> (THE SOPHIA OF JESUS CHRIST, page 218)

Just one more reference to the Sun symbolizing the Fire within:

> "The sun itself is symbolic of the heroic principle of all-seeing and all-knowing and the indwelling fire of life. The activation of this 'internal sun' we have called 'solarization' . . . " And, "Raw sun and domesticated fire are one in essence. As such the mastery of fire is the shaman's play with the Absolute."
>
> (SHAMAN, THE WOUNDED HEALER by Joan Halifax, page 25) (Edited)

Interestingly enough, the Sun was considered a Goddess in Oriental and pre-Christian times. The Vikings as well as the Celts worshipped the Sun as a goddess. The Egyptians identified the Sun with Immortality. (Walker) Later, it was asserted that the Sun was male to fit the religious patriarchal idea of the superior strength of the male.

Are you ready? Can you read these passages referring to Son as the Sun of man? The Son, Sun, Libido, Holy Spirit are all one and the same. The Sun gives us life. The Sun is all energy poured out upon us. We can also say this about our Son, our Inner Guide.

Aknaton, famous Pharaoh of Egypt, worshipped one God and his symbol of God was the Sun with rays ending in hands which reached down to the earth. Was he teaching about the Inner Son of man, the Sun, being our complete Energy?

With this background, let us go to the teaching.

In the first part of Chapter V Jesus had healed the man who had lain by the pool of Bethzatha for 38 years hoping to be healed in the water, but he could never get there in time. Jesus healed him on the Sabbath which was against Jewish Law. The Jews criticized the man and Jesus. Jesus replied, "My Father is working still, and I am working." (Verse 17) The Jews interpreted this as meaning that he considered himself equal with God so they wanted to kill him. Then Jesus gave the teaching on the Son and the Father.

The Father is that highest God, that Mighty Omnipresence, that Great Invisible. This term refers not to the God that humankind has devised to describe the All. Father refers to the Godhead. This was not the Yahweh of the Jews, the God of the Jews, but to that Indefinable Presence above and in all. It is indescribable—it is All.

In reading this scripture, put yourself in place of the Christ and realize that he was speaking from the Absolute level of Being. Imagine your own consciousness at that level and let us read it together.

> Verse 19: Truly, truly, I say to you, the Son (Sun) can do nothing of his own accord, but only what he sees the Father doing; for whatever he does the Son (Sun) does likewise.

When one reaches the mystic level of consciousness, this is the criteria for all action—doing the Father's Will; but being in a human body, most of us do not follow that Father all the time. The Son (Sun) within us is restless until It finds Oneness. Jesus Christ was at that Oneness; he was the Absolute; he was beyond the mystical level.

> Verse 20: For the Father loves the Son and shows him all that he himself is doing; and greater works than these will he show him that you may marvel.

Jesus the Christ demonstrated for us the possibilities for our own life. He said the Father loves our Son. The Father is love and that love pours into our Soul, into that Guardian, and is the Spark of Light which is that Spark of Love. Our recognition of that Love was one of Jesus' greatest teachings.

Verse 21 says the Father raises the dead and gives them the life and the Son also gives life. This refers to those human beings who are dead to their Inner Son, to their Inner Divinity. They are dead, but through the Son, the Divine Energy, through the Grace of the Father they are given life. That is how we are raised from the dead.

In Verse 22 we read that the Father does not judge but gives all judgment to the Son. When those who have been steeped in traditional Christian religion read the word "judgment" they may shudder, for they have been taught that they are sinful and will be judged at the last day. But judgment has alternative meanings.

Thus, for us, judgment includes Knowing, intuitive guidance, discrimination. True spiritual judgment is based on love. We have defined love as that Sophia that is our Holy Spirit. Judgment is our choice of going to Love for guidance. That lies within our consciousness. It comes from that Holy Spirit, that is the Son, and is our discriminating faculty. We judge, or evaluate, but do not condemn ourselves or others.

Jesus said that he who does not honor the Son does not honor the Father who sent him. (Verse 23) Is that why we have not honored the Son (Sun) within our own consciousness? We have not honored the Father, the Godhead. We have been stuck on narrowly defining that indefinable Godhead as our God. Here Jesus is trying to awaken us to our Son that is the Spark of the Godhead, a ray of the Sun.

In Verse 24 Jesus says:

> " . . . he who hears my word and believes him who sent me, has eternal life . . . he has passed from death to life."

The Supreme Love sends us to earth with a human form and a Spirit Core. We are sent here for a Purpose. Jesus knew his Purpose—his Son was doing the work that the Father sent him to do.

In Verse 25 he refers to the Son of God:

> Truly, truly, I say to you, the hour is coming, and now is, when the dead will hear the voice of the Son of God, and those who hear will live.

Much has been written and spoken on the difference between Son, Son of man, Son of God. I shall focus upon Son of God and would like to use Yogananda's definition of Son of God from his AUTOBIOGRAPHY OF A YOGI. (page 151 n.)

God the Son is the Christ Consciousness . . . existing within vibratory creation; this Christ Consciousness is the "only begotten" or sole reflection of the Uncreated Infinite."

This refers to John 1:18, "No one has ever seen God; the only Son, who is in the bosom of the Father, he has made him known." Our Son makes the Beloved known to us.

The Son of God, the Spirit, is unfettered by the human condition. "From the Father, comes the Son, as the Father's thought of his own being." (AION, Jung, p. 193) The Son of man is that Divine Energy functioning in the physical. The Son of God is the Divine Energy leading, guiding, healing. This describes our Oneness with the Godhead. "The Father and I are one," Jesus said or inferred.

Verse 27 says the Son has authority to execute judgment because he is the Son of man. The Son is that Spirit within which is the intuitive Knowing.

I like Verses 28 and 29 especially, for they have deep teaching for you and me. We who are on the path, search for direction.

> Do not marvel at this; for the hour is coming when all who are in the tombs will hear his voice and come forth, those who have done good, to the resurrection of life, and those who have done evil to the resurrection of judgment.

How often these verses have been used to strike fear into the hearts of the listeners. But listen now with your Third Ear.

Those who are entombed are those who are dead to the reactive, spiritual Kundalini Energy and understand their life as one long orgy of pain as well as pleasure through sex, materialism, self-indulgence and following the ways of the world. Jesus Christ predicts here that all *will*, not shall, hear this Voice some day and come forth from their dead state in the physical body. There is no life as long as we are having experiences that are putting the Son to death or have it in the tomb of our intellect. All addictions are putting this Son to death. Addictions are like a tomb and one is trying to fill the vacancy, the darkness of the tomb with food, sex, co-dependency, alcohol, drugs, etc. These will be overcome and life will result. Evil is defined as a separation from the Father's Guidance. Resurrection will come by listening to the Intuitive Knowing coming from the bosom of the Father through our own Son. Not judgment to Hell, but Judgment to Heaven.

Know that! Believe that! Love is teaching you now! Verse 30 acclaims that Jesus, the speaker, seeks not "my will but the will of him who sent me." We are all sent, and when we let go of our ego, our personal will, our intellectual choices, we will follow the Father's Will.

You may be wondering what all of this has to do with my Thesis. It *is* my Thesis. It is Knowing that the Holy Spirit, the Kundalini, the Sun of my Soul is from the Father and is lifting me out of the tomb of my physical body, my physical belief, to the resurrection of Enlightenment, of Life Eternal. The Son is the Christ and that Christ resides within me. Lifting that Christ to the Godhead consciousness takes physical, emotional, spiritual and intellectual balancing. The Son will do that as I recognize It and help It flow freely.

Jesus is very harsh sometimes with the non-believers. He is trying to awaken their Soul, the Spark within, and their recognition of their Holy Spirit. In Verse 37 he tells them the Truth: they have never heard the Father's voice, have never seen His form (their body as from the Father) and have not heard His Word in them because they have not recognized It. They do not believe that their Son was sent by the Father. He suggests that searching the scriptures for eternal life will be fruitless; but he says the scripture does bear witness to the Son, which they do not follow, in order to have life. In Verse 42 he says he knows that they do not have the love of God within them. This last seems very harsh, but when one depends on the scripture and not on the awareness of the Love of God within, one is lost. Verse 42 from the Jerusalem Bible reads: "You have no love of God in you." In other words, they are not recognizing that love of God within them. Being aware of this love and following His Grace is our Task. Not that there is no love of God in them, but that they do not love God. They do not recognize It.

Now most followers of traditional religion depend on that religion to "save" them. The scriptures, the religious authorities, the religious institution will save them, they are taught. They look to the outer for Heaven. They do not look to their own Inner Authority, the Love of God. Moses gave the Israelites a teaching from the outer which they needed at the level of their evolution. He gave it from within himself, but he realized that they needed an outer authority at that level of their belief in God. They had just come out of Egypt with the religious teaching of Isis and Osiris deep in their unconscious. But here Jesus was bringing the Jews a teaching that would lift them to a concentration on life, on Eternal Life, not on death. He said in this scripture that Moses wrote of him. He was referring to Moses' teaching on the High Energy that guided him, Moses, and the Israelites through the forty years desert experience. The Christ is what we call that Energy.

The last verse I want to discuss is Verse 44:

> How can you believe, who receive glory from one another and do not seek the glory that comes from the only God?

That glory is defined as splendor, celestial Bliss, light, wisdom. He points out that people receive glory from one another through association, through loving another. He is pointing out that the splendor is from God, from within. Glory, ecstasy, bliss may be experienced with a human encounter but becomes faint when compared to the Glory from an Enlightened State.

Paul gives us a definition of glory in II Corinthians 3:18:

> And we all, with unveiled face (fully alive to the Spirit) beholding the glory of the Lord, are being changed into his likeness from one degree of glory to another; for this comes from the Lord who is the Spirit. (Parentheses are mine)

We go from one degree of glory to another as we are being changed into God's likeness. Glory is the Golden Wedding Garment that is ours when we are at One with the God of All. Our Son has returned to the Sun, as the Egyptians taught. Our Spark has filled full our Soul and all is One.

This glory cannot be received from another. The potential for this glory can be awakened by the opening of the chakras by meditation, yoga practice, touch of a guru, but this is just the start. The Work must be done by us individually. The Work is described by Jesus the Christ, indeed was exemplified by him/her. Many of us have seen glory when we had a vision of the Light Presence. Jesus and Moses were both transfigured on a high state of consciousness (on a mountain). We, too, can "behold the glory of the Lord." This glory comes from the One and Only God, and our Christ brings this to us. Then we are Enlightened. We are transfigured.

Thus ends John 5. I would suggest that you study this chapter prayerfully, going within to your own Sun and listening to your intuition for what it can mean to you.

You are the Son from the Godhead. Jesus the Christ taught this great Truth. Accept and be resurrected from the tomb of intellectual, material death. The Light, the Glory of the Lord shines all about you and within. Know that the Great Being has sent you to lift the burden of others. Know!

This Chi, this Kundalini, this Ki which is taught about in Eastern religions, is the Son and we KNOW that it is in the Father. And so it is.

Chapter XII

THE KUNDALINI AS COMFORTER, HOLY SPIRIT, SPIRIT OF TRUTH AND THE APOSTLES BAPTISM

John 14:15-17, 20, 26; Mark 16:17, 18; Acts 1:1-19, Acts 2:1-7

When I start writing on this Title, I feel as though I am going into a strange, strange land. Bringing the Eastern and Western spiritual teaching into Oneness is like bringing my own Spark of the Divinity into Oneness with All There Is. It is awesome! I am Guided from Within to proceed.

In the Book of John we have so many lessons dealing with our Mystical Journey that we are often overwhelmed. We are also at a loss for words to describe these teachings. Jesus was at a loss for words also as he tried to explain the numinous experiences that were coming through his Father. He often spoke in parables to the populace in order to give a "down to earth" example of what great Truth he was teaching. To his disciples, who did understand somewhat, he used more abstract language. That is why his teachings for 2000 years have been interpreted in thousands of different ways. Now that we are also interpreting his words from the Thesis of the Kundalini being the Holy Spirit, we too may be misunderstood. But for those who are ready, our interpretation may bring them closer to that Oneness called Mystical. This is our prayer.

Let us now turn to John 14:15-17, 20, 26. I shall change the masculine pronoun to the feminine since I have established that the Spirit, the Kundalini, the Divine Energy, the Holy Spirit within our consciousness is feminine. Later we shall take you to Acts 1 and 2 for the account about the disciples receiving the Holy Spirit which

67

Jesus promised in John 14:16, 17. Remember that Jesus was speaking from the Christ when he made this promise.
John 14:15-17:

> If you love me you will keep my commandments. And I will pray the Father, and he will give you another Counselor, to be with you forever, even the Spirit of truth, whom the world cannot receive, because it neither sees (her) nor knows (her); you know (her) for (she) dwells with you and will be with you.

John 14:26:

> But the Counselor, the Holy Spirit, whom the Father will send in my name (Christ), (she) will teach you all things, and bring to your remembrance all that I have said to you. (Parenthesis mine)

These two references should open to our consciousness the Truth of our own Being. We accept these words as spoken specifically to us, Seekers on the Path. They were not spoken to just the heads of religious organizations but to Jesus' disciples which included the eleven apostles (Judas had left the group), and to you and me. These words are for each and every one of us.

In the King James Version of this scripture the words Comforter and Holy Ghost are used. According to Heline, VOLUME V, page 131, 132:

> The Comforter is the inner guidance which lighteth every man that cometh into the world, that light which so long is obscured by mortal mind but which when awakened leads to the fulfillment of all Truth. The Soul is the fountain of wisdom, the picture book of past ages. Through the awakened Christ power within, this storehouse of wisdom and understanding becomes accessible and its resources available for daily living. (NEW AGE BIBLE INTERPRETATION)

This is what the Mystics have been recording down through the ages and Jesus said it, "(she) shall teach you all things." Intuition is awakened when the Kundalini is flowing freely, not being depleted in physical activities, relationships and challenges of the world. This Inner Guidance, the Light, this Counselor, Holy Spirit, is the Source of all true creativity, and this is sent as the Christ from the Supreme One. It is a part of that Supreme One.

Jesus says the world cannot receive this Counselor, the Spirit of truth, because the world cannot see her nor know her but he says,

68

"you know (her) for (she) dwells with you, and will be in you." She will be in us when we recognize she has always been in us.

The world is the intellectual, judging, reasoning part of us. Those who are deeply controlled by their intellect think all of this "mystical stuff" is pure imagination. Indeed mysticism was put down strongly by the organized Christian world for years, calling it dangerous. Those who are into reasoning, logical living do not have the awareness of this Divine One that exists within each human consciousness. They do not recognize the Inner Guide for they are closed to It. But the spiritual Seeker Knows there is a Voice from the Inner Recesses of Being that has all the answers for the Journey back to the Godhead. Many Eastern religions teach this as a basic Truth as have the mystics both Christian and Kabbalist through the ages. A study of Teresa of Avila, Hildegard of Bingen and St. John of the Cross attest to It. (See THE WAY OF SPLENDOR by Edward Hoffman for Kabbalist Mysteries.)

John 16:13, 14 tells us that when we become conscious of this Spirit of Truth or It comes, we will be led to all Truth. Now to be led to all Truth is a high calling and it may take most of us many years or many lifetimes, but when that Spirit is at One with the Godhead where all Truth is, then we will pass It on to others in our various modes of creativity.

Verse 20 of John 14 reads:

In that day you will know that I am in my Father, and you in me, and I in you.

Jesus was speaking from his Christ Presence, from his Holy Spirit Presence. Our I AM is in the Father, the Godhead. When we have the experience of our own Holy Spirit, we recognize that It can only come from the Highest Reaches of Spiritual Knowing. Each of us is in the Christ (you in me), and the Christ, the Holy Spirit, the Spirit of Truth, is in us. When we receive the Holy Spirit Power we Know all of this Verse is Truth.

The Truth comes from the Knower of All Truth and when we are divinely guided to be at One with that Truth then Truth is ours. It is not our personal authority but the Authority of the Absolute that speaks through our Holy Spirit.

It is this Holy Spirit that Jesus said the Father (the Godhead) would give to each of the apostles and to us. This gift which we receive at conception in our mother's womb comes with us into our outer physical expression. Babies have an extremely high vibration of this Energy. Each one loses the awareness of It during the experience of earth living. When we recognize It we will raise It for spiritual Purposes.

The account of the apostles receiving the Holy Spirit baptism which Jesus Christ promised them is in Acts 1 and 2. When we read the description of them receiving the Comforter, the Counselor, the Spirit of Truth, the Holy Spirit which Jesus had promised them before his Crucifixion, we are made aware of It coming upon us also.

Acts 1:1-8 begins with a view of Jesus' presenting himself to the apostles during the forty days after his Resurrection and speaking to them of the Kingdom of God. Somehow, it is hinted that the visitation of the Holy Spirit is related to the Kingdom of God. He told them that in a few days they would be baptized by the Holy Spirit.

By the way, it is accepted by present day Bible scholars that Acts was written by Luke and not by Paul as we have often been taught. It emphasizes the coming of the work of the Holy Spirit.

In Acts 1:8 Jesus said that the apostles would receive power when the Holy Spirit came upon them and they should take his message to Jerusalem, Judea, Samaria and the ends of the earth. What a Commission! Note that he said the Holy Spirit would come upon them first. We need to have the experience of the Inner Christ before we can reach our Goal of serving our Purpose.

After he gave them these directions we have:

> And when he had said this, as they were looking on, he was lifted up, and a cloud took him out of their sight. (Verse 9)

The eleven apostles then went to the Upper Room where they were staying. They had an election to fill the vacancy left by Judas Iscariot, who had committed suicide. (Matthew 27:5) Matthias was elected. There were in attendance besides the apostles, women, Mary the mother of Jesus and his brothers. About 120 persons were in attendance.

Acts 2:1:

> When the day of Pentecost had come they were all together in one place.

This was at the time of the Harvest Festival of the Israelite religion, called the Pentecost. It followed fifty days after the Passover. The spiritual energy was high at this time of celebration. Humankind has always celebrated religious festivals which brings high consciousness to the participants.

In Acts 2:2-4 we have a description of the apostles receiving the Holy Spirit. Being given in very abstract terms, it can be interpreted in many ways and has been. I shall interpret from the Thesis which I am demonstrating. A few words, but the action it depicts has changed the consciousness of humankind for 2000 years.

> And suddenly a sound came from heaven like the rush of a mighty wind, and it filled all the house where they were sitting. And there appeared to them tongues as of fire, distributed and resting on each one of them. And they were all filled with the Holy Spirit and began to speak in other tongues, as the Spirit gave them utterance.

They were in a high state of consciousness. They had experienced Jesus' disappearance from them in what has been called the Ascension. They were ready. They believed his promise.

One may have an inkling, a hint of faith, that this Divine Energy is available and can be experienced. This often comes through the inspiration of a teacher, a guru, a vision or dream that opens the possibility of having this high spiritual experience. Many in revival services are so stimulated by seeing others respond to this ecstatic level of faith that they choose it also. Those who have this experience often do not understand it and may discount that it happened, for it can be frightening. In Jesus' last teaching he had told them that he must go away (John 16:7-11) for the Counselor to come to them. They had depended on him as long as he was there. This is also true for us. The visitation of the Holy Spirit is an Inner experience. It comes to us when we are turned within to our own consciousness and It is our Guide, Lover, Supporter.

This experience described in Acts 2 has been the basis for the development of much Christian creed on which many religious groups have been formed. The ecstatic experience that results from the touch of a leader, man or woman, in a religious setting can arouse this Energy. However, unless one builds on that experience, the results will slip away and the receiver will need the stimulus time after time for it to return. This is not what the apostles experienced, for after all, they had had the physical and spiritual Presence of Jesus the Christ and recognized the experience immediately. They were changed forever and took the message far and wide. Those who have a one time Rebirth experience and are awakened will stay in the adolescent stage of spiritual development without further Inner Work: prayer, meditation and living a Spirit-directed life.

In Acts 2:2 we have the "sound from heaven like a mighty wind, and it filled all the house where they were sitting." Those who have this high experience speak of a great ecstasy, a great spiritual experience like a wind filling their body, mind and soul. Wind is symbolic of Spirit. We know not where It comes from or where It goes. Room is symbolic of individual consciousness. So each one had this recognition of the Spirit filling them completely. There are many yogis who attest to a sound coming from within that is related to the Kundalini awakening. We must see this scripture as describing what happened within each apostle who was gathered in expectation in the Upper Room.

> Verse 3: There then appeared to them tongues as of fire, distributed and resting on each one of them.

The tongues of fire have been depicted in art as resting on the heads of those gathered in the Upper Room at Pentecost. We have noted previously that fire is symbolic of that high heat that moves up the spine and changes the cells of the body, the chakra centers and the consciousness of the devotee. This is the Kundalini Energy. We have testimony from Hildegard of Bingen, a German mystic of the 12th century:

> When I was 42 years and 7 months old, a burning light of tremendous brightness coming from heaven poured into my entire mind. Like a flame that does not burn but enkindles, it inflamed my entire heart and my entire breast, just like the sun that warms an object with its rays.
> (ILLUMINATIONS OF HILDEGARD OF BINGEN by Matthew Fox, page 9)

She wrote that she became ill, was healed by the creative act of writing her first book, SCIVIAS. Creativity is a great healer. As a result of this experience she discussed fire and painted many pictures surrounded by flames as testimony to the visitation of the Holy Spirit.

When we examine the course of the Kundalini from the base of the spine up the spine to the Seventh Chakra above the head we understand the King James Version of this scripture which indicates that flames sat upon them. The chakra was filled with Light, fire, flames. We can see a connection. Fire is also passion, emotional driving Force, the libido, Divine Energy.

Filled with the Holy Spirit brings an "out of this world" experience that cannot be described in words, or if described in words can only symbolize the ecstasy, the joy, the High that one has. The apostles were in an altered state.

Verse 4:

> And they were all filled with the Holy Spirit and began to speak in other tongues, as the Spirit gave them utterance.

This "speaking in tongues" has been a puzzle for many Christian religionists through the ages. Some believe that glossolalia (gift of tongues) is speaking as the apostles did on the day of Pentecost. Those churches that teach this believe that messages are coming from God for the congregants. Indeed, Paul speaks of this. Let us examine speaking in other tongues from the Holy Spirit.

All those in the Upper Room spoke in a different language or other tongues. In other words, they were so inspired that the words they spoke were filled with spiritual meaning that they had never experienced or understood before. When the Holy Spirit is consciously activated we change. Our whole outlook on what we have thought and spoken changes. Our Intuition is feeding our thoughts and our thoughts are expressed through the power of speech, by our tongue. The tongue is considered necessary for speech, for power of expression. These apostles, moved by the Holy Spirit, spoke in an entirely different language. They were Ecstatic at that moment. They were Enlightened. Perhaps they chanted in a language foreign to them but understood by their Intuition.

According to the Scripture a multitude gathered at the sound of the apostles speaking in various languages. They asked, "What does this mean?" And Peter, standing with the eleven, spoke.

Peter, the leader, has been designated as symbolizing the quality of Faith by Charles Fillmore. He has placed each of the Twelve Powers of man on various chakra centers. Faith he has placed in the center of the brain which is the location of the pineal and pituitary glands. According to Eastern religious teaching when these glands come together, Enlightenment is experienced. Faith was exemplified in Peter's first sermon. He was in an Enlightened state. He recognized the confusion of the multitude which had gathered as he spoke from Inspiration, from his Holy Spirit.

He quoted a long passage from Joel 2:28-32 where Joel prophesied this day would come when God would pour out His Spirit upon all flesh. Peter then testified about Jesus who was sent from God and who was crucified and killed but was raised up.

When the multitude heard his sermon they asked what they should do. His reply: "Repent, and be baptized every one of you in the name of Jesus Christ for the forgiveness of your sins; and you shall receive the gift of the Holy Spirit." (Acts 2:38) This is a major tenet of faith on which the Christian church was developed, and Peter, Faith, spoke it.

Acts 2:41 says that 3000 souls received his word and were baptized. Was it his word that he spoke that baptized them or was the Word, the Holy Spirit, activated in their souls and they were baptized? Pouring out of the Spirit on all flesh is happening today.

As an alternate interpretation, I should like to suggest that the number 3000 refers to the cells of the body that were baptized by the Christ within.

And thus it is. The Holy Spirit comes to us by Grace from the Godhead, Jesus' Father. The Holy Spirit is that Grace and is our soul's spark ready to bring us experiences of visions, prophecy, dreams that guide our Spiritual Journey. This Spirit is poured out upon men and women (Acts 2:17, 18) according to Peter's sermon quoting Joel. We also shall take it into the world, as Jesus Christ directed his apostles to do, in service to others. As we awaken to this Loving Energy, we will be raised to a new awareness and be baptized with the gift of the Holy Spirit.

It is by Grace that we are baptized. That Grace is Love from the Most High. We do not understand where it comes from. Jesus said:

> The wind blows where it wills, and you hear the sound of it, but you do not know whence it comes or whither it goes; so it is with everyone who is born of the Spirit. (John 3:8)

Grace abounds. "And with great power the apostles gave their testimony to the resurrection of the Lord Jesus, and great grace was upon them all." (Acts 4:33) We too have Grace upon us.

We must not be discouraged if we do not have the experience of the Holy Spirit at once, effortlessly, although it does come that quickly for some when they are open to It.

Eckhart says: "The fire of the Holy Spirit occurs not just once but little by little for the purpose of the soul's growth." (BREAK-THROUGH by Matthew Fox, page 373) We must not rush. Let the Grace of our Inner Spirit guide us and we will have our Rebirth, our Guidance, and our Soul will be totally impregnated with the Spirit and be carried back to Oneness, to Eternal Life, to the Kingdom of Heaven to be experienced here and now. We will be anointed with the oil of Truth, Wisdom, the Word and Creativity. Our Joy will never cease.

Sometimes we are most humble at the point of our greatest need. Then we are open to the Spirit. The disciples were open. They had just lost the Presence of their Guru. They needed guidance to carry out, "Go into all the world and preach the gospel to the whole creation." (Mark 16:15) They received the Guidance from their Holy Spirit. They were immediately filled and could speak the language of many nations, and they went into the world.

Our Joy comes to us as we receive that charge of Energy, we are open to our Purpose, and we go forth fulfilling It.

The Grace of God is active in our life and affairs many times without our recognition of It. It is more apparent after we have the awakening, the rebirth, by the Holy Spirit. But It, the Holy Spirit, is always within our consciousness awaiting our recognition.

When the Kundalini is flowing freely there are many positive results in our lives and the lives of others connected with us. Some of these are: the Spirit will be poured out on all flesh; prophecy, dreams, visions will be ours and we will pour out the Spirit on others (Joel 2:28, 29); pick up serpents (touching the Kundalini) (Mark 16:17, 18); witness for Christ (John 7:37-39); guided into Truth (John 16:13, 14); and words from the Holy Spirit are spoken (Luke 12:11, 12).

The apostles went forth converting, preaching and teaching. The first groups were very different from our present Christian church, but it grew out of the inspiration they received at Pentecost. The teaching has gone far and wide with many different interpretations which has separated the followers and has brought on a multitude of wars and killing of each other. Somehow the great message of Jesus the Christ on Love has been lost and then regained. The message has gone to Jerusalem (peace), Judea (praise), Samaria (intellect), earth (physical experience) within our own life. East and West have met and peace will be our inheritance.

Chapter XIII

PARABLES FROM JESUS THE CHRIST

We have now laid the groundwork for an understanding of Jesus' teaching. Knowing the Inner meaning of his statements has brought us to the point of applying them in our life. Describing the meaning of Kundalini, Holy Spirit, I AM, Son of man, Son of God, etc., has prepared us to discuss some parables. The Greek meaning of parable is to place beside for the purpose of comparison. The Christ, in explaining the use of the parable, told his disciples, "seeing, they may not see and hearing, they may not hear." Jesus used parables to teach his listeners who may be at diverse spiritual levels. Each heard or saw at their own level or consciousness.

A parable is a Wisdom teaching. Jesus used experiences of his listeners as a setting. He spoke of nature often—mustard seed, mountain, sea, sower, lost sheep, etc. He also used terms familiar to the merchants—talents, pounds, rich fool. He appealed to the poor about the lost coin, the treasure in the field, the empty house, the bond servant. All of these spoke to them at a deep level. Since these settings are not so familiar to us today we may be lost in trying to understand them as symbols, but they are applicable to our present mode of life.

We shall interpret a few of these parables that apply to our Thesis. We shall transform the figures of speech into the meaning as it applies to our Journey to Fullness of Knowing. Through this process I hope you, the reader, will learn to do the same with other parables that may interest you.

The Fig Tree

Matthew 21:17-22, Mark 11:12-14, 20-26

The first one I shall deal with may not be called a parable by some, but I believe Jesus was illustrating a deep Truth as he took action against the fig tree.

Matthew 21:17-22:

> And leaving them, he went out of the city to Bethany and lodged there. In the morning, as he was returning to the city, he was hungry. And seeing a fig tree by the wayside he went to it, and found nothing on it but leaves only. And he said to it, "May no fruit ever come from you again!" And the fig tree withered at once.

> When the disciples saw it they marveled, saying, "How did the fig tree wither at once?" And Jesus answered them, "Truly, I say to you, if you have faith and never doubt, you will not only do what has been done to the fig tree, but even if you say to this mountain, 'Be taken up and cast into the sea,' it will be done. And whatever you ask in prayer, you will receive, if you have faith."

The central figure is the fig tree. However, there are other words that give us our clue: fruit, faith, mountain, tree, sea. All of these have a bearing on our interpretation.

Jesus and the disciples (Mark 11:11) were coming from Bethany (house of figs). This title of the city came from the sound of sighing and wailing that the foliage of the trees made and the tears (gum) that were dropped. So Bethany is representative of that grieving which we are wanting to overcome to go to the city of peace, Jerusalem. This is done through following our Christ.

These two cities illustrate our human and spiritual Journey—out of sorrow into peace.

In Mark 11:12 we are told that Jesus was hungry—not physically hungry, for he had told his disciples at one point that he did not need to eat physical food for, "I have food to eat of which you do not know." (John 4:32) He had spiritual food, the Holy Spirit within. Our Christ is our spiritual food and the Fig Tree parable illustrates our misuse of that spiritual food.

Many have interpreted this parable as an illustration of Jesus' anger at a nonproducing tree and he could "zap" it with his word and look, and it would die. Oh, no. This has a deep, deep teaching. This is a parable, not to be taken literally, and deals with addictions of any kind.

Let us switch to the esoteric meaning. The fig tree gives us our clue to Jesus' explanation.

The tree symbolizes our physical spine up which the Divine Energy travels. The Tree of Life is an image of the Divine Essence moving up our spine through the trunk, and nerves and branches in the midst of the Garden, our body.

A tree grows from the union of earth and sun. This union of the masculine (sun) and feminine (earth) produces fruit—the chakras are opened and bearing flowers and fruit. Fruit is often used as a metaphor by Jesus. The sap, energy, produced the fruit. The sap is analogous to the blood which carries the Divine Energy throughout the body. If the sap of the tree rises without disease or interference it will produce flowers and fruit. If it is hindered from being fed by the sap, it dies. The blood carrying the Kundalini delivers this Divine Energy without interference unless hindered by our ego's demand or our physical or emotional demands for satisfaction.

The fig has been considered feminine. Dried, they were placed in Egyptian tombs as a symbol of the womb—rebirth was expected. The fig tree was worshipped as the residence of the Goddess in Egypt. Many believed that they had more sexual energy through eating the fig. By the way, since Adam and Eve used fig leaves to cover their nakedness, it is assumed by many that they ate a fig, not an apple, which aroused their sexual appetites. The forbidden fruit was the fig.

Our fig tree symbolizes the Divine Energy coursing up the spine but not producing spiritual results. There is no fruit, no enlightenment. The chakras are deprived, not open and bearing transformation.

Can you see? The Christ within us is hungry when this Energy is over-used for gratification of physical desires. The body will shrivel up with depletion of the Energy. We can restore It by attention to our Spirit within and the focus on spiritual transformation.

The disciples asked Jesus how the fig tree withered at once, and then Jesus gave them a lesson on faith.

We have not discussed faith to any extent because I felt it is a given. Most readers of this book know what faith means. It is faith that starts us on our Path. Faith can come by "hearing of the word"; seeing another person live by faith, indoctrination by religious teaching. However, real faith comes from our own conscious and unconscious awareness of Something Else that is a part of our life—indeed is our life—and through prayer and attention to it brings forth "fruits of the Spirit." Faith is the beginning of our Journey and eventually turns into Knowing. In Mark 11:24 we have this same statement, and the phrase "whatever you ask in prayer, believe that you have received it, and it will be yours." Believe that you will receive. That is faith.

In Matthew 21:21, referring to the fig tree, Jesus seems to be saying that to have faith and never doubt one can get rid of the reason for the death of our physical body and/or spiritual consciousness. I think he is teaching that misuse of the Feminine Energy, symbolized by the fig tree, has caused the nonproduction of the fruit. The misuse of this Spiritual Energy will cause all to wither. There are many who can attest to this who are caught up in addictions.

The Divine Energy needs attention, that is how we feed It. If our life is not producing fruits of the Spirit we will lose It in our conscious awareness, but It is always there awaiting our attention.

I realize this is very abstract, but read on.

Jesus spoke often of fruit as a simile for spiritual production. He said in John 15:2, "every branch of mine that bears no fruit, he (God) takes away, and every branch that does bear fruit he prunes, that it may bear more fruit." In Matthew 7:19 he says, "Every tree that does not bear good fruit is cut down and thrown into the fire." And Matthew 21:43, "Therefore, I tell you the kingdom of God will be taken from you and given to a nation (people) producing the fruits of it." And John 15:5: "He who abides in me, and I in him, he it is that bears much fruit, for apart from me you can do nothing."

Apart from the Holy Spirit, the Christ, the Kundalini, when not used for the advancement of our Sacred Consciousness, we do nothing—we will die either physically, emotionally, or mentally.

And why? Because we do not have faith, we doubt the love, the purity, the strength of the I AM, that is within waiting to be recognized and followed.

There are so many ways we misuse this Energy in trying to fulfill our conscious and unconscious desires: money, power, entertainment, attachment to pleasure of the senses. These often take first place in our desires. However, because we are dealing with a fig tree, a symbol of the use of our Divine Energy for sexual gratification, I shall discuss the use and misuse of It in that area of human life.

There are those who believe that Paul taught that the sex act should only be used for procreation. There are those religious authorities who teach that celibacy is necessary if one is to reach a high level of Enlightenment. Celibacy for priests is coming under much scrutiny as more and more priests in the Catholic Church are being accused of being pedophiles. Many are resigning in order to marry. Perhaps the rule for celibacy comes from the belief that Jesus was celibate, and from Paul's teaching as portrayed in the Bible.

The Protestant Church does not require celibacy of its ministers or preachers. However, some of these religious leaders have been accused of aberrant sexual activity—female and male leaders—with children and adult members of the church and outside of the church. The problem of expressing this Divine Energy in an acceptable manner is large. The religionist may have more difficulty with expressing it in a positive manner if they do not accept the teaching of the East on the activity of the Chi or Kundalini.

Indeed through the sex act one can reach that ecstatic experience that is similar to the Joy that is reached when the Kundalini brings together the pituitary and pineal glands in the brain and the seventh chakra explodes. The majority of humankind use this Energy for pleasure of the senses, however.

The problem with the latter choice is that overstimulation may deplete the nerves, cells and physical activity of the body and disease often comes on. Most scientists do not recognize that misuse of this Divine Energy depletes the immune system and venereal diseases as well as others can accrue. Now that AIDS has come on the scene we are reminded of "the branch withered and thrown into the fire." These diseases come to homosexual as well as heterosexual men and women, but the homosexual community seems harder hit. We know, of course, that a needle used for ingestion of a drug to feed another addiction also carries the virus.

This is true of heterosexual as well as homosexual men and women. The heterosexual seems to be freer now from any moral censorship if they change partners often trying to find that perfect partner who is seldom found. That perfect Partner lies within one's consciousness. That Partner is the feminine or masculine aspect of the psyche that needs to be balanced. Then the pure quality of the Ecstasy arises when Divine Energy finds Its partner with All That Is. Of course, I am not suggesting that this is a Path that will be chosen by everyone. It depends on one's conscious spiritual need. But the fact that the misuse of the Kundalini, Chi Energy may bring sorrow, withering of emotional flowers, and eventually deep depression—thrown into the fire of despondency—can bring one to their knees in deep surrender. Some psychologists are helping their clients out of this depressive state by teaching them about the Divine

Energy, how to meditate, and how to have the Spiritual experience they were born for.

How to handle our sexual urges can be one of a human being's major challenges. Our swing toward promiscuity has brought on a multitude of problems both social and medical. Many believe that most divorces are caused by one or the other or both partners having sexual relations outside the marriage. This does not mean that in the past this great urge was handled better. It is just more open now, but it has brought many new problems to our culture.

Whether one is homosexual, heterosexual or bisexual does not seem to make any difference. At the moment of this writing the spotlight is focused on the homosexual and bisexual. That will pass when society realizes that not one or the other expression of this Divine Energy is better. Our expression through the sex act often brings to us our greatest opportunity for bliss or to grow spiritually through the pain caused by the misuse.

The choice of celibacy seems too difficult unless one is centered on the Spiritual evolution to higher consciousness. Bringing together the masculine and feminine within the psyche of the individual will allow the experiencing of this Divine Energy in high ecstasy beyond any involvement with another human. Celibacy allows this Energy to accumulate, and celibacy allows for the high experience. The chakra flowers cannot be produced if too much of the Energy is being spilled in sexual gratification.

I should like to suggest that the homosexual is closer to the androgynous state, balanced in their feminine and masculine, than most heterosexuals, although of course this can happen whatever the sexual orientation we choose or chooses us. In the androgynous state of being this Energy could be used to serve humanity at a high level. The homosexual loves deeply and often is looking for a way to express it. Sometimes they turn to sex as a release. This need for release may turn into an addiction and their physical, psychological, spiritual and mental energies are depleted. If they change partners often the disturbance in their unconscious may bring an overwhelming sense of guilt, guilt over their deviancy from the so-called norm and their promiscuity. Also the dishonesty of "being in the closet" and pretending to be someone they are not depletes this Sacred Energy.

Guidance through teaching the world by their example of expressing androgyny would be profound. If the Divine Energy is scattered they may wither, be thrown into the fire of public criticism and may die, either psychologically or physically. Many burn in their own inner consciousness. That can be like Hell on earth, here and now. We have much to learn from each other, homosexual, heterosexual, and bisexual.

To become androgynous, according to Jung's teaching, one must clear the unconscious of blocks, meditate, turn within to the Presence which one really is, bring together the conscious and unconscious and thus overcome the division within brought about by concentration on either the feminine aspect of one's being or the masculine. The balancing of these two brings about androgyny. A definition of androgyny is, in its broadest sense, the One which contains the two: the male (andro) and the female (gyne).

Sex is a holy activity when used to express love and for generation of other human beings, but using this Serpent Energy to excess will prevent one's consciousness and body from regenerating. This was Jesus' teaching when referring to the fig tree. It is not the Path for everyone, turning to a serious spiritual expression of this Divine Energy, for many do not realize why they were born on planet earth. But it is an option. Understanding the need to balance the masculine and feminine energies helps.

Some "authorities" say that sex addiction shows a depletion of spiritual consciousness, since sex activity and spiritual activity are so close coming from the same energy, the *libido*. To grow spiritually, the mystics say, it is necessary for each to do the Work of attention to their Inner Spirit and this may require celibacy.

The Spirit is the Source of love and our need to express love in the sex act seems to be part of our human need as well as spiritual need, although we may not recognize it as such. For some this is a life-long choice. For others this hunger can be satisfied through meditation, attention to the Inner Spirit and by the circulation of the *Chi*, the *Kundalini* consciously. This can bring surcease from the hunger for sexual acrivity with another person and raise one's consciousness to an Enlightened level. Balancing the masculine and feminine energies will relieve the longing for a sex partner. When one has recognized this Inner Love, circulated It, and found Ecstasy in the Inner Self, the balance has been reached. Many men and women, even within marriage, are celibate and are having this High Ecstasy within. An inner balance, androgyny, makes celibacy an option. To live a celibate life without this balance is most difficult.

THE SECRET OF THE GOLDEN FLOWER, translated by Richard Wilhelm with a commentary by Carl Jung, speaks to this. It suggests that the use of this Divine Energy for procreation hinders the unfolding of the Golden Flower, or what is called by Hindus, the Thousand Petal Lotus.

But it is transformation not repression it is suggesting. Sexual impulses can be turned inward instead of outward and thus a rebirth can occur.

The Tibetan and Taoist's teaching on Tantra sex allows the participants to conserve as much as possible of the seminal fluid, both in men and women, by having an internal experience of bringing together the Yin and Yang to nourish each other. The Taoist believes that then the seminal essence would ascend to rejuvenate and revivify the upper brain. All of these methods seem very foreign to the Westerner, but have proved effective if celibacy seems to be an impossible choice.

The method is to learn to circulate this Energy through the body, up the spine, and down the front of the body by different breathing exercises, chanting of mantras, etc. THE SECRET OF THE GOLDEN FLOWER gives instructions for this process. This is an Inner Spiritual experience and brings Ecstasy beyond any experience in sex between two individuals.

Celibacy does not mean that the individual does not love others. On, no. This Energy is Love and will be expressed more easily and at a deeper level to many, many persons. This is what Jesus taught us. This Energy of Love can then more readily be released to give food to the hungry, drink to the thirsty, welcome to the stranger, clothing to the naked, and visiting the sick and those in prison. (See Matthew 25:35, 36.) Jesus said when you do these acts to another you "do them to me," the King, the Queen, the Christ of our Soul. In service to our brothers and sisters this Divine Energy is scattered to the needy on this planet. That includes the world of nature and the Earth. When we reach this point we are regenerated.

Regeneration needs the new-birth and is the change and filling of the Soul by the Spirit, Grace of God. Fillmore defines it as: the unification of Spirit, soul, and body in spiritual Oneness.

In Matthew 19:28 Jesus says, "Verily, I say unto you, that ye which have followed me, in the regeneration when the Son of man shall sit in the throne of his glory, ye also shall sit upon the twelve thrones, judging the twelve tribes of Israel." (KJV) Thus, regeneration will follow when our Son, our Holy Spirit, sits in the thrown (the crown chakra) and glory shall be ours. That is regeneration and is called by many other terms—individuation, enlightenment, nirvana. The twelve thrones may refer to the twelve chakra centers throughout the etheric body which are filled and vibrating with the Son (Christ). The twelve thrones also have an esoteric meaning. See THE TWELVE POWERS OF MAN by Charles Fillmore.

There are other physical, psychological desires to which we are attached, of course.

As mentioned before in Matthew 21:21, Jesus gives the answer to how to overcome addictions to any physical, sense desire that may bring death to the Tree of Life. He said that if one has faith and never doubts one can say to this "mountain," "Be taken up and cast into the sea" and it will be done. "And whatever you ask in prayer, you will receive, if you have faith." (Verse 22)

Beginning with Mark 11:20b, which relates this same parable about the fig tree, it is reported that when the disciples and Jesus came by the fig tree that he had caused to wither and in answer to their question said: "Have faith in God, have no doubt in one's heart but say to the mountain, 'Be taken up and cast into the sea.'" He also said to ask in prayer, believing that you have received it and it will be yours. He added that forgiveness was necessary so that "your Father, also, who is in Heaven may forgive you your trespasses." Father is our I AM, our Life, our Divine Energy.

To cast a mountain into a literal sea is not what he meant, of course. It is to cast a habit that is as big as a mountain in our conscious and unconscious thought, in our physical and psychological desires, into the sea, into the Creative Force, the Spirit, and it can be done. The Twelve Step Program of Alcoholics Anonymous is an aid to so many and the "mountain" is submerged, eliminated from ruining lives. It teaches the confession that there is a Higher Power than one's small self and then to humbly pray for God to remove all shortcomings, the addiction is moved into the sea.

Eventually, however, one must depend on one's own Spirit for healing and not be so dependent on the group to heal addictions.

What a wonderful teaching for all of us, for we all have some propensity, some mountain, that we think cannot be overcome, cleansed, turned around, but here we are told to have faith in God, pray, forgive, and the mountain (problem) will be transformed into a blessing. So our problem whether it is sexual addiction or any other addiction will disappear into the Spirit, the Universal Energy we call God.

Another way to explain this is that we lift the addiction to the height of spiritual consciousness, high on the mountain of spiritual consciousness, forgive our small self as well as others. Then it, the addiction, is baptized in the Spirit, the Eternal, the Sea.

In closing this section on a very sensitive issue, I should like to draw to the attention of those who are deep into meditation, chanting, yoga and Eastern practices for physical or spiritual development, that they are activating their own Divine Energy and this may pose problems if they are not aware of what is happening.

If one is participating in these activities, the Kundalini may be raised to one center or another and get "stuck" there. This may cause great upset especially if too much energy is in the lower three chakras. This Energy when "stuck" at the second chakra center, the sex organ center, may induce much craving for sexual release. To move it further up the spine can alleviate this condition. David A. Cooper in his book, SILENCE, SIMPLICITY, AND SOLITUDE, says, "It is not all uncommon to see people 'stuck' in the second chakra, obsessed with sexuality, or in the third chakra, on a personal power trip. The primeval nature of the first three chakras is substantial." (page 246) Moving this Energy to the heart chakra level will often take care of this problem.

Such negative results are attested to also by Gopi Krishna in his book, KUNDALINI, THE EVOLUTIONARY ENERGY IN MAN. One may need a teacher who understands the action of this Energy. Sometimes the overwhelming desire for sexual activity, he says, seems to be the only release for the strong Energy. This choice may bring psychological problems or physical problems which can cause great anguish. Education from the East is needed, he states, to help those Searchers understand what is happening. The Spirit, the Serpent Energy moves and may be misused if not understood. Understanding and realizing that spiritual upliftment can heal, will bring balance.

The fig tree that does not produce the fruit to fulfill the hunger and balance of our physical, emotional, mental and spiritual being, may die. We are warned by our Teacher, Jesus Christ. If you have a mountain to move into the sea, know that there is Guidance through faith in God for it to happen. Producing fruits of the Spirit is your Destiny.

The Ten Virgins, Foolish and Wise

Matthew 25: 1-13

This parable has been the foundation for various teachings: a description of the natural use of women's energy; as an example of the lack of consciousness in women; and a teaching on being prepared. Some see it as the background for the history of womankind who have not expressed their individual talents, but have sacrificed their Self to the needs of the males in their society. It has been used as an illustration for those who are not "saved" and those who are. For the purpose of my Thesis, however, I see this as illustrative of our lack of Light in order to have the Mystic Marriage. When we are fully *Enlight*, we reach that level of awareness of our Divinity which has been called by various names:

Guatama the Buddha called it Nirvana; Paul called it Christ or the Spirit of God; Mohammed, Gabriel; Dante, Beatrice; Walt Whitman, My Soul; Jesus, the Kingdom of God or the Kingdom of Heaven.

Since this parable starts with,

> Then the Kingdom of Heaven shall be compared to ten maidens who took their lamps and went to meet the bridegroom.   (Verse 1)

We shall discuss the Kingdom of Heaven first.

As I am sure I have mentioned, the Kingdom of Heaven is a state of consciousness, here and now. It is not in a far-off place in the sky, in the heavens. The Kingdom of Heaven, Jesus said, is within you. The Kingdom of Heaven is that ecstatic experience of Oneness when the Kundalini energy fills all the cells of the body, all the brain waves, all the consciousness and we are lifted into True Reality. This has been named the Mystic Marriage by Christian mystics throughout the ages. Jesus spoke at great length about what, where, and how to enter the Kingdom of Heaven. It comes to each of us in different ways and is a part of the Perennial Philosophy—has always been and is in every religious teaching under various names.

The ten maidens were called virgins in many scriptures. It fills my purpose to consider them virgins.

We are all virginal when we start a serious Spiritual Journey. We each have our own individual experience of the Beginning. We are born virginal in our realization of the Light, but we soon lose it by physical living. The Christian church, as well as other religions, base their belief on the dogma that the Founder was born of a virgin. This is a tenet of their faith, but that teaching has been described as a virgin from the physical standpoint. I should like to discuss how, from our spiritual virginity, we can be wed to that One that is deeply Known but seldom experienced. The Spouse to be, is the bridegroom mentioned in this scripture and is the Invisible Unknown.

We have dwelt at length on the feminine aspect of the Holy Spirit, the Divine Energy. This is within each of us; this is the Virginal Spirit that will become the bride of the Bridegroom, All That Is, sometime, in some lifetime. That is the reason for this teaching from Jesus the Christ. The virgin can be seen as the Soul that is seeking Marriage; as the Soul prepared to receive the Fullness of the Divine. This the five prepared virgins experienced. Five virgins did not; they were unprepared when the call came. But I am getting ahead of the parable.

In Verse 1 we have mention of lamps. A lamp is a symbol of the chakra center that carries the Light. Seven chakras exist, but the Light may diminish in them if not given attention. Jesus referred to the lamp of the body as the single eye in Matthew 6:22. This may refer to the Third Eye, the location of the sixth chakra which when filled with Light lifts one to that Transcendence of Being. Barbara Walker sees the lamp as a symbol of Enlightenment and Corinne Heline says that the Illumined One always carries a lamp within. Each of us has these lamps that need refilling in order for Light to prevail in our body and consciousness. We can be Enlightened.

Matthew 25:2-5:

> Five of them were foolish, and five were wise. For when the foolish took their lamps, they took no oil with them; but the wise took flasks of oil with their lamps. As the bridegroom was delayed, they all slumbered and slept.

Note that five of the virgins were foolish and took no oil to replenish the fuel for the Light, for their lamps. The five wise virgins took oil with their lamps.

The numbers ten and five may refer to the senses according to some interpretations. In one case the five senses were fed spiritual Light, were regenerated to be used for spiritual growth. The other five senses were used in the darkness of ignorance for self-gratification, for generation, for pleasure of the senses. These were the foolish ones. This is a viable interpretation also.

Ten, however, is a symbol of Unity. The potential for all of the feminine aspects of our personality to have the Divine Marriage is within us, but when our five-sense personality is not evolved to multisensory personality we are found lacking. The multisensory personality is regenerated, is above the sensory.

Oil is a light symbol. It refers to the Christ. Anointment with oil (olive) in the religious circles was and is related to the passing on of spiritual energy to the Initiate.

So our ten virgins, open and receptive to the Christ consciousness, go to the Sacred Wedding. Now it was nighttime, a time of darkness, which indicates a state of consciousness—darkness, Dark Night of the Soul. This parable is teaching us that out of the dark times of our life we may be invited to the Wedding. We can go to the Marriage if we have prepared our body and consciousness.

Often we sleep through this time of our life. Often we can see nothing but darkness, but out of that darkness can come light, for the Bridegroom, although seemingly detained (Verse 5), will come. The ten virgins slumbered and waited.

At midnight, which symbolizes a temporal turning point, a turn around when the Light begins to creep into the darkness, the shout went up,

"Behold the bridegroom! Come out to meet him!"   (Verse 6)

Now each of us, if we are seeking our Oneness, hear that call. Most of the time it is not like a shout but is the "still small voice," but that "still small voice" can feel like a shout, for we are awakened from our deep sleep.

Verse 7, 8 is the result:

Then all those maidens rose and trimmed their lamps. And the foolish said to the wise, "Give us some of your oil for our lamps are going out."

The wise virgins said, "No," and told them to go buy some for themselves.

Notice, the maidens (the virgins) with consciousness of their appointment, rose and trimmed their lamps. It is when we awaken to our feminine task, both men and women, of going to the Bridegroom that we put out some effort to trim our lamps or pour light into our chakra centers in order to be at that high state of awareness—wide awake.

It takes some effort on *our* part to be ready for the Mystic Marriage.

Many have Enlightening experiences without logically choosing them. In fact, the Light experience comes to most of us without any expectation. Many of us slumber and sleep until the call comes forth and then we awaken to our Destiny and prepare for it by deep meditation, reading of spiritual books, finding a Teacher, living a life guided by that Inner Spirit and devoting our lives to attaining that Enlightenment that our Soul longs for. All of this prepares us. We are ready if we are wise. We have the Light needed, we have the oil (consciousness) needed to make the last step through the door into the Bridal Chamber. That is, we are one of the five wise virgins.

The suddenness of this Light experience and unexpectedness of it is pointed out by Jesus in the last line of the parable,

> Watch therefore, for you know neither the day nor the hour.
>
> (Verse 13)

In Mark 13:35-37 Jesus speaks to this:

> Watch, therefore—for you do not know when the master of the house (consciousness) will come, in the evening, at midnight, or at cockcrow, or in the morning—lest he come suddenly and find you asleep. And what I say to you I say to all: Watch.

And in Luke 12:40:

> You also must be ready; for the Son of man is coming at an unexpected hour.

The Son of man is that Christ within our consciousness, the Master of our Spiritual Consciousness.

Now all the maidens trimmed their lamps. All of us in one way or another are preparing our Self for its Marriage with Universal Consciousness. Our Self is moving in that direction although we may be unconscious of it. We are all preparing for It through whatever choices we make, either physically, spiritually, or emotionally. Our choice of religious belief is part of that trimming. The Master may come before we are fully prepared to go in to the Wedding.

What do we do when the lamp is lacking in oil to keep it burning? Sometimes we turn to a guru, a preacher, a priest, a loved one, our family, our spouse, our children to give us the oil, the fuel for our final step into the Light. We depend on others to give us this high spiritual experience. But Jesus' parable says, "It cannot be. You must fill your lamps yourself. You cannot borrow from another."

We must be spiritually vigilant, and wait. This may be an unconscious vigilance or a conscious one. Sometimes we do not realize we are ready, as attested to by mystics throughout the ages. (See Maurice Bucke's COSMIC CONSCIOUSNESS.) No one else can give us the fuel for our lamps, for our chakras, for our consciousness. That is our responsibility. If we are foolish we ask others for our oil.

Sometimes, however, if we are not wise we may loan our oil, too much of it, to another and thus deplete our supply. We have been taught that to love another we must be willing to give of our abundance. However, Jesus is teaching here that each one is responsible for supplying their own energy for the lighting of their lamps, the chakras. Each one of us must become separate and develop our own spiritual consciousness and, interestingly enough, when we do that we are One with all others, for our Spirit and theirs is One coming forth from the same Godhead. However, if we give too much of our own oil away we shall not enter into Enlightenment. The wise virgins demonstrate this.

Men and women have done this for ages. Society has required women to do so more often than men. Just now are women beginning to keep their spiritual power for their own expression. They have often supported men and children and forgotten their own needs. Most of that support has been in terms of physical and emotional needs. Most of that support has depleted their own ability to express who they are—children of God with a spiritual purpose. Serving others did not help those served either. Up to a point, when a woman chooses marriage and children, she will need to serve through love; but when that service weakens the energy of the ones served because they are not doing for themselves what they are capable of, she is giving away too much of her Light, or oil. Co-dependency is built on this theory. That is changing, and the "wise virgin" is serving her own Inner Light through personal expression of her God-given gifts. I recognize that men are also using their Energy to support their family as well as their own physical desires. This can be to excess, and they do not have the time or energy to fill their own spiritual needs. They, too, are giving away too much oil.

If the wise virgins had given to the foolish virgins they would not have been able to go in to the Bridegroom. We, both men and women, must protect our own supply of Divine Energy. This may mean giving up excessive attachment of family, children, spouse. We release them to their own Journey. Remember, the beginning of the parable points out that we are talking about the Kingdom of Heaven Consciousness.

We can encourage those who are too dependent on us to go get their own "oil" and pay whatever price is required; and that will mature them in their Search.

While the foolish maidens went to buy oil the Bridegroom came; the wise went in to the Marriage Feast and the door was shut. When the foolish returned they called to the Lord to open the door, but he replied, "Truly, I say to you, I do not know you." (Verse 12)

This lack of Kundalini Energy can keep us from entering Life Eternal or the Kingdom of Heaven. Remember, Jesus said, "The *Kingdom of Heaven* shall be compared to ten virgins who took their lamps and went to meet the bridegroom."

This Divine Energy within is now being recognized by those in the West who are in the forefront of the spiritual evolution of humankind. In Bill Moyer's TV program (HEALING AND THE MIND, 1993, PBS) the first segment was on the use of the *Chi* by the Chinese for healing, for health, for long life, and for spiritual needs This *Chi* is the Kundalini. The medical profession is realizing the use of acupuncture and massage, which removes blocks to the Chi's flow, as necessary for health of the body. Religionists of the East and the mid-East teach of the spiritual connection this Divine Energy has with our consciousness evolution. This Chi is the oil for the chakras.

Now, with our world-wide network of TV, radio, and fax, this knowledge is becoming part of the consciousness of those who are interested in spiritual evolution in the West. Yoga is being encouraged in the West to reduce tension and stress. This activates the Kundalini and will eventually lead the participant to the realization of this Energy coursing through the body. This will add to their spiritual search or to an understanding of what is "going on." All is in Divine Order. We cannot borrow from the East, however. The pilgrims in the West need to supply their own oil.

We are ready. We are the wise maidens. We have waited a long time in the darkness of Aristotle's intellectual choices, but now humankind's consciousness is rising and more and more are turning within for Guidance in contemplation, meditation, centering prayer. The physical and emotional needs of humankind is bringing about this change. We are obtaining our own oil. The need for peace and preservation of our planet is a strong movement of spiritual consciousness, which is our support, our food, our physical being.

The parable of the foolish and wise virgins fills us all with wonder and awe. What a wonderful teaching coming from the Father of Lights, the Christ within Jesus. That Light is our Light, but we must fuel It with attention. Forethought will keep our chakras bright and burning. Our body and consciousness will be transformed in the Light and we will enter the door to the Marriage Feast with the Lord. The door will not be shut against us. We will be known and accepted into the Kingdom of Heaven. I would remind you again:

> Watch therefore, for you know neither the day nor the hour wherein the Son of man cometh. (Verse 13, KJV)

We have that Kundalini Energy, that oil, within our soul, mind and body, all One, and it circulates throughout our Being. We are One with That Which Is. This you will KNOW. Let your lamps be filled with the Holy Spirit and your Light will shine and give glory to the Father within your Heaven. This is the Kingdom.

The Prodigal Son

Luke 15:11-32

This most important parable has become a part of the Christian race consciousness. The term Prodigal Son does not appear in the Bible. It is also told with some variation in the Buddhist Lotus Sutra 4. It has Truth that touches us all at a deep level for it tells "our Story." There are few human beings who do not sink to a low level of consciousness of *Who* they are before they reverse their lives, their choices. There are some who do not turn around in this lifetime, I suppose, but through Grace they turn in another lifetime, in another dimension. This is the loving Way of that Presence we have named God. Each of us have this Hope, this Grace, surrounding us and leading us however unconscious we may be of It.

This was certainly true of me. Each depth of despair I reached, I turned to the intellect and some prayer to lift me up, set me on my feet, show me my path; but I had to reach the depths of emotional pain before I started to seriously return to my Father/Mother of Lights. The intellect lifted me for years, but the emotional pain could not be assuaged by the intellect, and thus I chose the Spiritual Path. I returned to the Christ. For some it comes more easily but for most of us, if we allow the pain to register on our conscious mind, we look for something or someone, God, or our Inner Spirit, to help us. It makes all the difference *which* we choose, intellect or Spirit. We have further suffering or great Joy, depending on our choice.

The reason I have chosen this parable to demonstrate my Thesis is found in Luke 15:13;

> And not many days after the younger son gathered all together, and took his journey into a far country, and there he wasted his substance with riotous living.   (KJV)

Other Bibles use the words fortune, money, property, wealth for *substance*. I shall interpret *substance* as spiritual essence, living energy, divine substance. That is our greatest wealth and we waste it for many years in a far country away from the Spirit, in riotous living. This *substance* is the Energy underlying the reality of all things.

Substance is the libido. In a later verse substance is connected with harlots. It is the life of the Holy Spirit, it is the Kundalini. It can be used for generation and/or regeneration.

An entire chapter could be written on the meaning of *substance*. Researchers on spiritual and religious matters have defined it. Some of these are:

Omnipresent Spirit, God, Spiritual Energy, Kingdom of Heaven, Christ Within, Life of body and spirit, Eternal Truth, Life, Love, Spirit, Life Force. It is that Inner Spark on which all depends. I shall use these definitions in my exposition.

Now that we have established the definition of *substance* let us go to the parable.

Before Jesus told this parable he had mentioned the parables of the Lost Sheep and the Lost Coin to answer the Pharisees who had condemned him for receiving sinners and eating with them. Those parables emphasized repentance and forgiveness as does the parable of the Prodigal Son.

A quick review follows:

A man had two sons. The younger asked for his inheritance and the father divided his "living" between the two sons. The younger one took his share of the "living" (substance or Energy) and went into a "far country" and used up all of it in "loose living." When he had spent all, he joined someone of that "far country" and was sent to feed swine. (Pork was avoided for food, for it was a theriomorphized god, a wild animal in Egyptian religion.) This was the lowest of lowest of occupations and one could be contaminated by the association. He was not given anything for his work and he was reduced to eating pods that the swine ate. These were beans from the locust tree.

He finally awoke, he came to his Self, he remembered his father. He determined to go to his father, repentant, and say, "Father, I have sinned against heaven and before you. I am no longer worthy to be called your son; treat me as one of your hired servants." (Verses 18,19)

Here we have a change of mind, a change of direction; repentance for mistakes, humility and loss of pride. There was a faith that his father would accept him or he would not have returned.

"He arose and came to his father." (Verse 20) This indicates our own guidance, and when we turn to the Holy Spirit, our Mother, our Christ, we come up higher, we "arise."

He did not know how his father would receive him, but when his father saw him returning he had "compassion, and ran and embraced and kissed him" and the son asked for forgiveness. He said he had sinned against heaven (that high level of Ecstasy that comes with Oneness with the Father of All) and with deep humility he said, "I am no longer worthy to be called your son." (Verse 21)

This complete loss of pride, ego, is necessary for us if we are to return to our Home. Until we reach the "bottom" we are not ready to reverse our life and return to the Spirit. The addict has attested to this as well as many mystics who say they "hit bottom" before they had the Divine Light experience. When we let go of all and turn to *All*, our life will again be filled with Light.

The father then asked that the best robe be brought and placed on the returned son, and a ring be placed on his hand, and shoes on his feet. The fatted calf was to be killed and eaten and celebration was to occur. Said the father, "For this my son was dead and is alive again; he was lost and is found."

Returning to the I AM can be a painful Journey. The younger son was in a "far country" and had to overcome many blocks to return, but his father's forgiveness and welcome gave him the treatment of royalty. In our interpretation he had come back to the Kingdom. He was received with love. The fine robe symbolizes the Light Body. The ring, a circle, is used as a symbol of betrothal or marriage. The shoes separated him from earth living, gave protection for his understanding; and the calf, although interpreted as physical food, might symbolize getting rid of the old state of consciousness. Remember the Golden Calf that Aaron set up for the Israelites to worship, which was destroyed by Moses? The Golden

Calf was a symbol of a deity in their old home, Egypt. So the younger son had returned from a "far country" away from the Spirit. He returned to a state of spiritual consciousness and left the old.

His father's reception was filled with Love and Grace.

Let us speak of Grace, to be reassured that Grace abounds no matter what our crime or mistake (called sin by many). It gives us strength. That Grace is not in a far-off place where God is said to reside. That Grace is within our Soul. That Grace is Love and accompanies us always. That Grace is what turns us around. That Grace offers us hope that we can get out of the quagmire of our wasted life. That Grace is the father spoken of in the parable. That Grace is the Holy Spirit. That Grace is personal and impersonal. We always are accompanied by Grace.

Talking of Grace reminds me of that famous verse from Psalms 81:16 which mentions "I would feed you with the finest wheat, and with *honey from the rock* I would satisfy you." An unlikely place to find honey we might think. This honey is that Grace. This honey feeds us in our desert place as we go to the Holy Land, the Kingdom of Heaven consciousness. This honey seems like a miracle, as does the Love and Grace of our Exalted One.

The elder son who had stayed with the father and seemed to be perfect, was not. This may be true of us also, for sometimes pride comes forth when we believe we have served our God, followed Guidance from the church teaching or the Bible or our Inner Self, and yet have not been given such a celebration as the so-called sinner, the returning son, is given. In Verses 26-30 his objections are told. He refused to go into the celebration and was angry. Perhaps he was afraid he would lose his place of being first in the father's house.

We are reminded of a line from Jesus' teaching:

> For everyone who exalts himself will be humbled; and he who humbles himself will be exalted. (Luke 14:11)

When the father came and entreated the elder son to come to the celebration, the son said:

> Lo, these many years I have served you, and I never disobeyed your command; yet you never gave me a kid, that I might make merry with my friends. But when this son of yours came, who has devoured your living (substance) with harlots, you killed for him the fatted calf! (Luke 15:29, 30)

This was his human side speaking, his human side of jealousy, accusation; fear and envy got in the way. We, too, are human and Divine.

We go in and out of the Kingdom consciousness. Sometimes we do not understand the challenges our brothers have gone through, for we have not experienced them. We may doubt our status with the Father of All. We are still immature. We have obeyed the Guidance from our Spirit, but we are still subject to our humanness. We should remember that we are with Jesus' Father always, for we can never leave that Beloved completely. We are that Beloved. We are not totally conscious of It. We are always with It and It with us.

The elder son who had always stayed with the father had not learned how to forgive yet and was incensed over the celebration that was prepared for the return of the younger brother. When we do not go astray we often think we are better than our brothers and sisters. This elder brother was near the father but touched by the small self. When he saw the celebration for the younger brother he lost touch with the Self and was jealous.

In recounting his brother's sins he mentioned, "But when this son of yours came, who has devoured your living (substance) with harlots, you killed for him the fatted calf."

The "living" that is expended on harlots is explained in Proverbs 29:3, "He who loves wisdom makes his father glad, but one who keeps company with harlots squanders his *substance*." Loving Wisdom is loving the Holy Spirit, the Kundalini, the feminine aspect of our psyche. Squandering that Energy is the life of physical pleasure and attachment to desires that separate us from the Beloved.

Note that Verse 13 of the King James Version changes "living" to "substance" which was wasted in loose living with harlots.

The younger son's substance, which was really his father's, may have been used for sexual activities in the temple, since the Canaanite's worship included prostitution with men and women. This worship was dedicated to the fertility gods. Perhaps these were the harlots he spent his Divine substance on. To the Israelites the ritual prostitution was a dark sin. Of course, we prostitute our spirit in many ways besides sex.

Let us interpret harlots as prostituting our Energy in physical living. So often we are not aware of our wasting this Divine Energy in our physical duties, our work, our desires. We may spend this Divine Energy in our responsibilities to family and society. This is all good up to a point; but we may find ourselves in a "far country" away from our realization of Divinity. Using this Divine Energy in consuming physical pleasure causes a loss of our Divine Substance also.

Mental illness, physical illness, loss of mental capabilities, loss of material possessions and relationships, and maybe loss of our physical life, can result when we are using up this Kundalini Divine Energy for earth living primarily. When we awaken, we hunger for our spiritual infilling. We will leave these attachments, which are so much less than the Joy and Ecstasy of the Spirit, at some time, in some lifetime.

So our elder brother, the consciousness within us which we believe we have made sacred, may have developed spiritual pride which causes us to be unforgiving and we may not rejoice when we see another pilgrim, who has made many mistakes, turn around and return to their Sacred One. We may not be joyful at the other's return. Our need is to forgive and have compassion for the returnee.

The father answered the elder son:

> Son, you are always with me, and all that is mine is yours. It was fitting to make merry and be glad, for this your brother was dead, and is alive, he was lost and is found. (Verse 31, 32)

What a shock to the eldest son this would have been since for the Jews the first son as the only son. Jesus is teaching the value of all sons and daughters.

The father points out that the younger brother had been dead but was now alive, was lost and now is found. That is an expression of Grace, of Love. The older brother needed this teaching. He was learning about forgiveness for another's loss of direction.

Now the prodigal will use the father's "living," the Energy of the Holy Spirit, in the Eternal One's House. That is the Return.

From a psychological viewpoint we might interpret this parable as saying something about the trinity that resides within our own psyche.

The elder brother could symbolize our conscious mind. The younger brother our unconscious and the Father the Superconscious. We go in and out of one or the other of these three when they are separated. When the conscious mind is most egotistical and unforgiving, the unconscious may bring up a memory of how we were not perfect as we thought. Consciousness of our Spirit, our Superconscious, is always there but our unconscious may be in a far country and filled with the husks of the pigs, symbolizing negativities and misuse of our Energy.

Until this unconscious is cleared by dream interpretation, meditation, prayer, spiritual counseling and/or psychotherapy based on spiritual needs, it cannot join the Superconsciousness. These two then joined to the conscious mind bring Wholeness.

The metaphysical practice of Denial and Affirmation helps, but without "turning around" and letting the dark side come up to conscious thought, repenting and returning, we cannot reach Oneness with the Superconscious. This clearing of the Shadow in our unconscious will allow Oneness of all three.

Returning to the Spirit within, called Father by Jesus, is the real cure. Then the Kingdom of Heaven can be experienced. Intuitive Knowing results; we are cleansed and we experience Divine Ecstasy and clear Spiritual Guidance for our Journey.

This younger son, the unconscious, admitted his mistakes and the unconscious was cleansed and presented no block to Oneness. The robe of Light (Enlightenment), the ring of gold (Marriage) and shoes (understanding) resulted. The Return was celebrated. His Spirit (substance) was retained for a royal place in his Father's house.

When we let go of the hunger which has been feeding on the husks of our selfish inclinations (pigs) we gain repentance, humility, and a turning away from our defeatist thoughts and feelings. We take the step to Return and "go Home." The Prodigal came to himSelf and Returned.

The hope and faith and the Knowing of the love of our God can turn us around. It takes courage, also, and although the youngest son did not have friends to encourage him, he did not need them. For us also it is an individual Journey and our decision to take it is primary.

Jesus the Christ said that he came to seek and to save the lost. The higher Self is always waiting for our Return. The small self often wastes the life force in filling physical needs, but the "still, small voice" calls. Earth living may be experienced to the full before we turn to our ladder of Evolution and climb it. The great Eternal Love of God, of which our Inner Christ is a spark, is waiting to welcome us Home, and we are of the Royal Family.

Humility is ours as we start our Path and reach the Kingdom and we are welcomed.

In Ephesians 5:14 we find our final Guidance:

> Awake, O sleeper, and arise from the dead, and Christ shall give you light.

And So It Is!!

There is more, so much more, that we could learn from other of Jesus' parables but we will stop here and encourage the reader to interpret others from their own Light of Self-consciousness.

The parable like the myth, story, and fairy tale, is to bring awareness of our own personality problems and solutions, and to ultimately reach a state of Completion. Jesus' parables were for those who had "ears to hear and eyes to see." They can all be applied to our individual Spiritual Path and they came from our greatest Teacher. Most parables are connected with the Path to the Kingdom of Heaven.

Living the spiritual life in our body of Light is our Purpose. The parables give us many clues as to how to do just that.

Seek out your parable. Find that one that speaks most directly to your need, your circumstance, your mystery. Meditate on it. Ask questions of your own personal Spirit. Listen and learn more about your Path to the Kingdom. Much instruction for our Christing lies in our unconscious. Find your parable and listen. You will be enriched spiritually, materially and psychologically!

Now let us go to the Divine Subject: Spiritual Healing.

Chapter XIV

SPIRITUAL HEALINGS

Throughout the ages there has always been interest in spiritual healing, or healings without the use of pills, ointments or the surgical knife. Indeed, during the time of Jesus there were not available some of these methods of healing although there were probably herbal healings. In some societies the Shaman did the healing. Jesus is considered a Shaman by many. As a result the healings performed by Jesus, as related in the Gospels, were an exciting transformation for his disciples and the multitudes that followed him. Many of them were healed.

How Jesus healed has been an enigma to many, especially those in our Western world who do not honor the idea of the Spirit, the Kundalini, Chi, being the healing agent used by Jesus. The healings reported were done by touch, use of his spittle, saying a few words and looking at the ill person. Even touching the fringe of his garment had healed a woman. (Matthew 9:20, 21) He healed from a distance also when asked to do so by one who was closely connected to the sick person. The faith of the requestor was important. Many put these accounts in the category of fable, but many have used these methods and have been successful in healing.

The Old Testament has few accounts of healing. The New Testament has more. Jesus brought to the attention of the Jewish and Gentile world of that day the feminine energy that resides within each one of us and can bring health to ourselves as well as to others.

The spiritual healing movement in the United States was enhanced by the experiences and teachings of Phineas P. Quimby, who practiced in Maine in the early nineteenth century. Mary Baker Eddy founded the Christian Science organization. The methods she taught, while similar to the accounts of Jesus' method, relied on prayer, consciousness raising, affirmations, denials and the feeling of love moving from the consciousness of the healer to the one who needed healing. Use of medical doctors was discouraged.

During this period there were other healers who relied on various other methods of healing. Those methods came from a religious setting. Most mainline Protestant churches have not emphasized healing as a part of their task, although following the teachings of Jesus and Paul did bring healing, both physically and psychologically, to many. The Catholic Church to a large extent devoted their teaching on healing to the confessional and following the various worship requirements.

Before we discuss the healings performed by Jesus in which he used the Divine Energy, I should like to review briefly other healing philosophies and techniques of several groups. These will include Kahuna healing, Shamanism, healing with Chi, Sufi healing, Siddha healing. All of these in one way or another give evidence to my Thesis that this Holy Spirit, Divine Energy, called by other names, is the healing factor and the one that Jesus used.

Over all, one of the primary requirements of each of these methods was faith in the healer. This faith in the healer was undergirded by faith in a God or Being that encompassed all. This faith was in the Mighty Omnipresence called by various names and worshipped in various ways. Likewise with Jesus' healings, he often said, "Your faith has made you whole."

Many of these healings encompassed physical as well as psychological diseases, although the latter were not understood as thought deviation or psychological. The idea of the unconscious being the source of disease did not come to the consciousness of humanity until Sigmund Freud brought it forward. In spite of this, the release of demons from the consciousness of the insane was practiced in Bible times.

Let us start with Kahuna healing which sprang from what we now call Hawaii or the Polynesian Islands. My sources are KAHUNA HEALING by Serge King, and THE HUNA CODE IN RELIGIONS by Max Freedom Long. This will be a brief description. You may want to research in these books or others.

According to that belief, the usual cause of illness was the blocking of the path of the Energy of the High Self. When blocks were removed the healing occurred. The healing factor was called *mana* which in our terms is the Life Force, the Holy Spirit. The cord, the spinal cord, had to be cleansed so that the *mana* could flow to the affected part. Laying on of hands, visualizing the person as healed and other methods were used to unblock the flow.

Water was often used as part of the healing process. The water could be charged with *mana* by the healer's hands, breath and concentration of energy. Also, the eyes carry a high level of *mana*. It is pointed out that cold thoughts must be exchanged for a positive emotion of love if the healing is to be successful. Again, they emphasized that illness or distortion of any kind resulted from interference with the flow of Source Energy or *mana*. This the healer restored in the healee with his/her *mana*. The result of the healing continued as the patient used techniques that opened the flow of *mana* in their body and brain. The Hula dance is one such technique. To "hula" is to raise the sacred flame.

As an aside, we know Tai Chi from Taoism is a dance of the body and spirit to be used for the same reason. Also, aerobic dancing and Sufi dancing have the same good as the Hula dance. We have ignored the value of sacred dance in our Western religions although it is being restored now.

According to Muktananda, of the Siddha movement, in WHERE ARE YOU GOING, physical diseases, as well as such negative qualities as anger, lethargy, envy and greed are caused by impurities blocking the flow of prana (life force) in the nadis (channels). (See page 73.)

Swami Muktananda, from the lineage of Siddhas, comes from Hindu background, and established Siddha teaching centers all over the world. His teaching and presence have opened thousands of people to their own inner divinity by his touch, glance, love, mantra chanting, and visualization. The head of this organization now that Muktananda is deceased, is Gurumai Chidvilasananda. Major Centers are in South Fallsburg, NY and Ganeshpuri, India.

Muktananda taught that the activated Kundalini dispels disease and keeps one healthy. Our thoughts are directly related to this Energy and can block its flow. These thoughts pass to the prana (Energy) and directly into the bloodstream and the entire body is affected. When the name of God is evoked this thought flows through the bloodstream and can bring healing. It lifts the Kundalini; it arises. The toxins in the blood are removed, the prana freed, and the mind is cleared from negative emotions. (See page 90.) Note the use of prana and kundalini as the same Energy.

A rush of Ecstasy results from the lifting of the Kundalini. The heart is affected with the love that is the Ecstasy.

This goes along with Paul's statement, "If the Spirit of him who raised Jesus from the dead dwells in you, he who raised Christ Jesus from the dead will give life to your mortal bodies also through his Spirit which dwells in you." (Romans 8:11) That Spirit, that Christ, is the Kundalini, and when we are ill we are as dead. That Christ raises us up.

Muktananda teaches that meditation, chanting, various asanas (bodily postures) will unfold the Shakti or Kundalini Energy. He stresses the guru's grace as a means of activating this healing Energy.

This is a brief description of Muktananda's teaching, but follows or leads my conclusion that Jesus Christ, our Guru, used these same methods, as well as others, to heal.

According to Sufi teaching, the Philosopher's Stone spoken of and taught of by the Sufis, as well as the Alchemists in Europe and China, is a state of mind, concentrated on by the healer from his Inner Being and then transmitted to the patient by means of his thought. This Stone is the Force and Essence of life. (See THE SUFIS by Idries Shah.)

The Sufi Dance is for healing and raising the Divine Energy to the head and throughout the body.

I shall touch very briefly on Shamanism which seems to fit our Thesis. According to John Sanford in HEALING AND WHOLE-NESS, the Shaman was the primitive healer. Sanford points out that the major religions all over the world are shamanistic. The healing skill comes from the ecstasy within the Shaman. (We have some examples of this ecstatic experience in the Bible: Moses on Mt. Horeb; the visions of Ezekiel and Daniel; Jesus on the Mount of Transfiguration.) The Shaman can affect the unconscious of the sick person. It was believed that if soul (spirit) and body were sepa-rated, illness occurred and perhaps death. The Shaman's duty was to return the soul to the body in order to effect a cure.

Jesus as a type of Shaman healed the sick, raised the dead, seemed to be on familiar terms with the spirits that invaded a sick one (they spoke to him), and His death, resurrection and ascension fit the Shaman paradigm. Today we would call the demons the Shadow or complexes in the unconscious.

Sanford points out that the ultimate source of healing lie beyond human personality and exist in the Divine Source. Health and wholeness lie within the patient and not within the therapist. (San-ford was an Episcopal priest and is now a Jungian therapist and author.)

For the Chinese the Sacred Energy is called Chi. They believe that illness comes as a result of the *yin* and the *yang*, feminine and masculine energies, being out of balance. The *yin* and the *yang*, according to Taoism, are in charge of the world. When working together and in harmony, the individual as well as the Universe is in balance. For health, for healing, balancing of the Energy is necessary.

Disease and pain block the flow of the Energy. Using acupuncture, herbal remedies, massage will bring healing. Practicing Tai Chi, an exercise, balances the Energy as well as increases it. The oldsters of China practice it "religiously."

Chi, according to them, is physical, spiritual and mental. When in balance the Tao, the Way, has been achieved.

Now let us turn to some teaching on healing from Emma Curtis Hopkins, Carl Jung, Yogananda, Corinne Heline and Charles Fillmore. Some of these teachers do not mention the Divine Energy as the healing agent. Alternative methods of healing were taught by them and most of them believed that they were following the example of Jesus Christ. I will make these brief as more extensive discourses are readily available through their writings.

In Volume V of Heline's NEW AGE BIBLE INTERPRETATION there is an extensive Chapter on Jesus' healing ministry. These are a few statements from that Chapter:

> Practitioners of all schools of healing realize the curative power of faith . . . and permanent healing is effected . . . in the realization of the power of Spirit to heal. (page 20)

> Jesus worked always with the inner man, demanding that the spirit exert its God-given powers . . . (page 21)

> Throughout the pages of the Bible the teaching is explicit that sin or wrong doing is the direct cause of disease. (page 30)

She points out that to be completely healed the soul lesson must be learned by the healed one. Jesus often said after a healing, "Go and sin no more."

Lifting the feminine pole, she says, is necessary for healing and making it upright with the masculine in equality. Thus she is saying what Jung says about the necessity of balancing the feminine and masculine within our psyche to bring wholeness, health, individuation.

The great mystic Emma Curtis Hopkins wrote that God is health. She suggests many avenues of healing in her book, SCIEN-

TIFIC CHRISTIAN MENTAL PRACTICE. She does not use the Hindu words in discussing the need for a free flow of Energy, but the implication is there. She does mention the "fine, fleet life-fire that streams through all the world." She points out repeatedly that feelings of love are necessary if the healer is to be successful.

One of the New Thought philosophies is called Unity. It was started by Charles Fillmore and his wife Myrtle and was based on the spiritual healing activity. Throughout his writing, the movement of the Divine Energy is stressed although not always interpreted as the Kundalini by many of its modern teachers and ministers. In his book THE TWELVE POWERS OF MAN this teaching is hidden except to the reader who is open and profoundly moved by the Truth of the Divine Energy in their own consciousness and body.

In the 12th chapter entitled *Generative Life* Fillmore speaks often of the "holy stream of life" and that it brings ecstasy to the meditator. He suggests that thoughts and emotions send messages to the body through the nerve cables (nadis?) that lead from the ganglionic centers. Those centers are the chakra centers in Hindu language. The real serum, he says, that will heal is the new lifestream opened to us by Jesus' teaching and example.

According to Fillmore, the ability to pick up the Life Current and through It to vitalize the body is based on the right relation of ideas, thoughts and words. These start currents of energy and produce health. This, he says, was and is the healing method of Jesus.

Two other organized New Thought groups also practice spiritual healing: Divine Science founded by Nona Brooks and Malinda Cramer, both of whom were healed by the Spirit; and Religions Science founded by Ernest Holmes. Their healing practices are similar to Unity's with some variation. (There are many other groups devoted to spiritual healing which I have not named.)

Carl Jung, whom you must be familiar with by now, taught that a healthy body and psyche depended on a healthy unconscious and conscious mind. Therefore, much of his teaching deals with the cleansing of the unconscious by various methods, some of which are dream interpretation, active imagination, and meditation. Although I cannot point to a specific teaching on the Divine Energy as the healing factor, he wrote the Commentary to Richard Wilhelm's translation of THE SECRET OF THE GOLDEN FLOWER, and incorporated Eastern religious teaching in many of his works.

Jung mentions in this Commentary on the GOLDEN FLOWER that the Golden Flower is the light, and the light of heaven is the

Tao. In this book the Golden Flower is the Energy called light. He comments that it rotates according to its own law and a cramp in the unconscious or conscious mind blocks its release. When unblocked the light then flows freely. Thus healing of thoughts and feelings occur. This unblocking of the unconscious is one of Jung's major teachings, of course.

One last reference to Hindu Teacher, Yogananda, who combined Hindu and Christian teaching. I shall quote from his book, THE SECOND COMING OF CHRIST. On page 195 he says, "As acids can dissolve a record, so the mental and psychological grooves in the brain cells of an error-stricken individual can be obliterated by the transmission of Life Force."

And, "Jesus signified his complete unity with God, and that he was free of illusive egotism. He could say to the sick, 'Thy sins be forgiven thee by God.' This God is the Holy Spirit or Son and It does the healing."

With this foundation, let us now move to discussing some of the healings Jesus performed. We will touch only a few that clearly demonstrate our Thesis: That the Divine Energy of Jesus, the Father of Jesus, performed the healings by arousing the Holy Spirit in the ill one, which cleared the body and mind of infirmities.

Before we continue, however, let us bring to your remembrance the greatest Laws of all, according to Jesus. This is the Law of Love, and was the healing agent that he used: "The first is 'Hear, O Israel: The Lord our God, the Lord is one; and you shall love the Lord your God with all your heart, and with all your soul, and with all your mind, and with all your strength.' The second is this, 'You shall love your neighbor as yourself.' There is no other commandment greater than these." (Mark 12:29-31)

It was these Laws that he demonstrated in all his reported teachings and healings. This Law of Love refers directly to the Kundalini, to the Holy Spirit, to the Life Force, to the Divine Energy for THAT is Life and Love. That is why humankind is so confused about Love—what it is, where it is, how it is to be used, how it is to be passed on to others as well as the entire world; for we have separated, at least the Western religion, the Inner Self, the Divine Energy from Love. Love has been left in the dust. We have tried to admit it and use it for our human self, for our own benefit as well as, sometimes haltingly, for others.

The Kingdom of Heaven is the Kingdom of Love. Jesus Christ's main teaching was on that Kingdom that is within the human consciousness. All that Jesus is reported to have done was based on Love.

Let us not forget the second Law—love another as we love our Self. Now many have interpreted that to mean to love our small self as we love another's small self, but the Self referred to is our own Divine Energy we call Life. Our direction is to love another's Self, another's Life and Love, as we Love our Lord, our God, in our own consciousness.

Love of everyone—beggar, thief, men who were controlled by demons, the prostitute, the sinner—was Jesus the Christ's way and example. On Love were all of his teachings and healings based. Love is God and God is Love, however, inadequate those terms are.

How to love is another question. I am convinced that when the individual activates this Divine Energy or It is activated by Grace, then one can truly love and make Love the foundation of his/her life. This Love brings Ecstasy, Enlightenment and Transformation of all human qualities into God Consciousness.

Chapter XV

JESUS' HEALINGS

We shall approach this topic by our usual method of seeing truth behind the written word that has a deeper meaning for each one of us. We so often read about these sicknesses and healings recorded in the Gospels from a literal viewpoint and we say, "Oh, that does not apply to me, that is not my problem." But there is deep truth in each one for you and me. Blindness, deafness, leprosy, possession by demons, a withered hand, paralysis in spiritual progress, raising from "deadness" to the Spirit—all of these and many more were healed by Jesus speaking a word, or touching, or looking into the eyes, or using his saliva and clay. But what do these mean to us in our modern day of *materia medica*? Let us see if we can find the answer.

There are 23 specific cases of Jesus' healings not counting the raising from the dead. I should point out that the word pain does not appear. The disease is described but no mention of pain. Could this be our clue that these healings did not just deal with physical ailments? Could they relate to a lack of our realization of the Spirit?

This brings us to a major question. What is it that we are all seeking spiritually, psychologically and physically? Is it not wholeness or as some say "holiness"? And how do we go about obtaining the answer to that deep longing? The answer to that question makes all the difference. Usually it is by various activities in the outer. But what is our real longing? I believe it is to be at One with the Holy Spirit, Love, Joy—that which lies within us and is all around us. That is the real healing. That Holy Spirit, that Kundalini, that lies waiting for our attention is the real healer. It was the Christ that did the healings recorded in the New Testament, the Christ through the consciousness of Jesus. It is that Christ, that Holy Spirit, that heals. It is not the physical that causes the illness or the healing. It is that Divine Energy that heals and if it is blocked the healing cannot take place. There are those who believe that Karma from a past life causes the illness, but the healing is in the now.

Bringing this Energy into balance is the task of the medical doctor as well as the spiritual healer. It is allowing that Divine Energy to flow freely in love that brings our healing. It is this love that the healer, be they spiritual or material healers, must demonstrate.

We need the complete attention of the healer, centered on our need, to arouse that Healing Energy. This may come from faith in a medical doctor, a chiropractor, an Ayurveda healer, an herbologist, a spiritual healer. When we have faith in the healer, it works. But there is more, and often Jesus said: "Go and sin no more," as well as "Your faith has made you whole." Faith relaxes the tension and the Kundalini flows freely. Faith in God's love heals. We can choose which method is most acceptable to us at the time.

Now, if we take the teaching of the Christ through Jesus as our Guide, we need to understand from a deep level the lessons we are to learn. One of his teachings was for the healed one to "tell no man." Now why? Wouldn't we want others to know that we have healed someone, or that we are healed? No. He said, tell no one. These healings were to be kept secret. Why?

Because when one's Divine Energy is flowing freely, secrecy is needed. Stabilizing the healing would make it last. Talking about the healing, bragging about it, celebrating it would diminish the Energy, and as Jesus taught in another scripture, the second condition would be worse than the first. "Tell no man," an order to many that he healed. The Vitality that the Christ had given to arouse the Energy in the sick one would be lost if they talked about it. Also, many would discount that the person was really healed. That could displace some of the faith of the one healed.

Now we must remember that Love was Jesus Christ's major teaching along with the Kingdom of Heaven. He did not put the Kingdom in another dimension. He said it was within, and that Love and Kingdom are experienced when we are healed—healed of that which separates us. When our health, physical and psychological, is restored by a sympathetic, loving, forgiving and understanding healer, in whom we believe, we are healed instantly. All of these Jesus Christ demonstrated.

Those who have interpreted Jesus' method of healing have come up with other alternative methods through the ages. I shall not go into those as they are recorded in other books dealing with the healing methods taught. However, thought control may appear to be primary. And also a feeling of love is necessary if the healing is to be successful. Now it would appear that Jesus healed in this way. But the element left out in discussions of most healing methods is recognition of the lifting of the Divine Energy within the seeker for healing to be complete. This is a vital part of all of Jesus' healings, I believe. The healings were not just physical but deeply spiritual; also psychological as when he released the seekers from demonic possession.

Today we have many medical doctors who are combining the scientific as well as the intuitive spiritual practice of healing and are being most successful. However, most medical doctors treat the symptoms and do not bother with the cause. There is a movement toward holistic medicine which takes into consideration the whole person—body, mind, emotions and spirit. I believe this is the medicine of the future. It takes courage for a doctor to step out of the safe circle of scientific research and reach up to the spiritual; but more and more doctors will be doing this as the scientific methods of healing fail.

Jesus did just this. Evidently the tried and true methods of healing in his day were not successful. He used the Holy Spirit method and it worked. He was derided for it, but his KNOWING that he was following the Father's Will directed him to continue on.

Let us go now to a few accounts of Jesus' healings.

Healing the Withered Hand

Luke 6:6-10; Matthew 12:9-13; Mark 3:1-5

We shall use the account given in Luke 6:6-10 for our discussion.

Jesus had gone to the synagogue on the sabbath where he had taught. A man was there whose right hand was withered. The scribes and the Pharisees were always trying to catch Jesus in the breaking of the Law and wondered if he would heal on the sabbath, their holy day, so they could accuse him of breaking the Law. He knew their thoughts and saw this as a divine appointment to teach a deep lesson.

He said to the man with the withered hand:

"Come and stand here." (Verse 8)

The man came to him.
Then Jesus asked the spectators:

111

"I ask you is it lawful on the sabbath to do good or to do harm, to save life or to destroy it?"

(Verse 9)

He looked at them and said to the man:

"Stretch out your hand." He did so and his hand was restored.

(Verse 10)

Now how did Jesus heal the withered hand? How did he heal without herbs, chemicals, scalpel? He had none of these for any of his healings. He did touch at times. Was this the same as acupuncture which removes the blocks to the Divine Energy. He did speak the Word: "Be healed!" He did use clay from the earth at times and also recommended washing with water. How did he perform his healings?

I do not pretend to know the complete answer, but these are some suggestions:

First, by implication, he asked the man if he wanted to be healed, as he requested him to come to him. The man evidently had faith in Jesus or he would not have come. So faith was necessary and the healing power of the Christ was necessary.

Then Jesus asked: Is it Lawful to do good on the sabbath? This was posed to the onlookers as well as the man to be healed. Obviously Jesus believed that the Law applied in this case.

He then directed the man to stretch out his hand. Again, the man had faith. He did so and his hand was restored.

Our focus is on healing the withered hand. Note that it was the right hand. The right hand has more power than the left—for most people it is more active than the left. It is the hand that gives, that heals, that blesses. What does this mean for us?

Jesus Christ healed with touch, word, looking with love. Healings came from his Divine Energy which was at such a high level that anyone within hearing or seeing was healed. He healed thousands of the sick, so the Bible reports.

There are many lessons in this account for us.

Remember Jesus was in the synagogue—a holy place of worship. Was he overcome by the Law made by man? No. He knew there was a healing element in the man with the withered hand and within himself that could heal.

The hand symbolizes holding, giving, touching, reaching out, service, blessing, clapping for Joy, and, yes, cruel acts can be performed by it. We should ask ourself if our own hand is withered.

This hand was restored. How can we restore ours? First, we must be in a Holy Place, the Inner Sanctum of our Christ. Then we must have faith in the healing power of our Holy Spirit, our Kundalini. Courage to overcome adherence to the Law of the intellect (Pharisees), symbolizing the scientific medical practice and recommendations is needed. Then to allow the Christ to direct us to "Hold out your hand" and receive the Divine Energy which will heal our thinking, our body, and our emotions. Sometimes we need a healing to our withholding of good to ourselves and to our fellow man. Prayer, faith, meditation and the action of the freed Holy Spirit does the healing.

The Christ restored the hand. The Divine Energy from Jesus awakened the man's Divine Energy and restored it. Let us not forget that the hand's perfect activity is dependent on love. The hand was healed when the Energy was not blocked. Love restores. Our healing will take place in our center of worship. That worship is on the Inner Secret Place of our Soul. There abides healing.

Is your right hand withered? Is giving to your Self and to others withered? An important question. If so, turn within and be healed.

Healing Peter's Mother-In-Law

Matthew 8:14, 15

This is a very short account of the healing of Peter's mother-in-law.

And when Jesus entered Peter's house, he saw his mother-in-law lying sick with fever; he touched her hand, and the fever left her; and she rose and served him.

When we read this from a physical healing direction it does not have the impact that it does if taken from the esoteric level.

Taking it literally is possible but we would have to ask why Jesus touched her hand to effect the healing of the fever. Why was the hand chosen? We might suggest that her fever was the result of a blockage of the Energy in that part of her body. How did he know where to touch? Of course, Jesus Christ was clairvoyant which he demonstrated many times. This comes to the Seeker who is at a high level of Knowing. Maybe she had used too much Energy in serving and thus the Energy was deficient in that part of her body. Her reason for being was to serve, it would appear. In any case she was healed and the next verse gives an account of Jesus healing many others including casting out spirits with a word.

Let us now see this account as symbolizing something within Peter's consciousness or our own consciousness. Let us see Peter as sick with fever.

Peter symbolizes faith. His house symbolizes his body or consciousness. The feminine within him was out of balance. Being touched by Christ consciousness healed this imbalance. The passion of his emotions was neutralized and the fire within, the Divine Energy, was channeled to allow him to rise, to get up from his misdirected position and serve the Spirit of all Knowing, the Christ. Thus Peter or faith was lifted up by the touch of the Christ.

So it can be with us also. The feminine may be sick within us. It needs healing before we can find our true Self, express our faith fully. We are in the age of Feminine Ascendancy. Men and women alike are experiencing it.

This Energy, symbolized by the mother, serves us and we serve it as our thoughts are centered on our positive, loving, joyous feelings and we are free from the blockage of the Energy. It is active. The blood then carries the Energy throughout the body and all dis–ease disappears. We are healed by the touch of the Christ, and our faith is made whole by the balancing of the masculine and the feminine.

Healing the Blind Man

John 9:1-7, 35-39

Let us turn now to an account of Jesus healing a blind man. There are several accounts of Jesus' healing the blind and interestingly enough they are all blind *men*. I want to make clear here that blindness in the outer vision may be the result of our misusing or violating some law of nature that we may be totally unaware of. As for any disease that a person may have, no guilt should follow but much spiritual development can occur if we use our physical disabilities as a positive opportunity to turn within and be healed throughout our body, soul, mind with the Spirit. We can be blind to the Spirit—this may be our blindness.

The account of the blind man found in John 9:1-7 is my choice and John 9:35-39 is an account of the disbelief of the Pharisees (the intellect) that the blindness was healed.

Jesus, as the account goes, saw a man blind from birth. His disciples asked who had sinned since the man was born blind—the man or his parents. (There is ample evidence in the Gospels that reincarnation and karma were accepted then.) In answer to their questions, Jesus said:

> It was not that this man sinned, or his parents, but that the works of God might be made manifest in him. (Verse 3)

This is the teaching for us. God's healing is made manifest in us with the touch of the Christ, the Divine Energy.

Jesus added: "As long as I am in the world, I am the light of the world." (Verse 5) Remember I AM was his real Being, God incarnate, the Holy Spirit, which is true of us also.

Jesus spat on the ground, "made clay (mud) of the spittle and anointed the man's eyes with the clay." Then he told him to go wash in the pool of Siloam. (I would remind you that the Lord God, according to Genesis, formed man from the "clay" of the earth. Clay is considered feminine as it comes from earth, the feminine.) The spittle carried the Chi. The man washed in the pool and came back able to see.

Siloam refers to Shiloh which was a sacred place with a pool of water. Washing in water, being sprinkled with water, has carried a connotation of healing for many religions. Water is often a symbol for Spirit, or for the cleansing aspect of the Sacred Energy. Baptism in water or immersion in water is a sacred ceremony for believing Christians and other religionists.

In accounts of the Aesculapiads which the Greeks and Romans designated as healing centers, washing in water was an important part of the healing. They believed that the healing came from the direct intervention of their god in the soul of the patient. But first the patient must have a dream that indicated that he/she should go to the healing center and then when accepted through purification by confession and ritual bathing in a pool or stream near the healing temple, he/she was placed in a room and slept and dreamed. The dream brought the healing. Notice that each person was involved in his own healing. (See John Sanford's HEALING AND WHOLENESS.)

Belief in the effectiveness of baptism by water may be necessary if some are to be cleansed. Thus Jesus sent the man to wash away any belief in his blindness, any belief in his guilt, any belief that he inherited the condition. The water, the Spirit, did the final work. Evidently his attachment to his blindness was so great that it took something besides clay and spittle to effect his healing. The clay and spittle, both of which contained Vital Energy, started the process.

115

In another account found in Mark 7:31-35, Jesus is said to have used his saliva to heal an impediment in a man's speech. Could this be saying that an impediment in speech indicates a blockage of the Divine Energy? Do we stop the flow of the Divine Energy by neglecting or refusing to speak, write, draw, sculpt, invent from that inspiration?

Let us now go to the esoteric teaching contained in the healing of the blind man. In Verse 5, Jesus said, "I am the light of the world." In answer to his disciple's question about the reason for the man's blindness, "I AM the Light." That Kundalini Energy is Light, Life, Love. Those all are healing Energies. Christ brought Light. And what is Light? Well, not even our scientists are sure, but we KNOW—Light is Spirit, Light is within each of us. Light is the Divine Energy within and without. Yogis say that seeing Inner Light is part of their Journey. We are filled with Light and it needs releasing into our thoughts, our body, our feelings. Light takes away our blindness to our Inner Knowing. Enlightenment is the word we use to name our totality of Light experience. I AM, the Spirit within, is Light.

But we are often blind, so often. We are blind to who we really are. Not a beggar but a Royal One. The Kingdom of Heaven is ours for the asking. When we "see" the Light we have that Kingdom. It lies dormant within us until we are awakened by the touch of Light, by the touch of a Light Being, or a guru, or understanding with our heart the healing Light that lies within us. To be healed, we need to wash away the debris which may lie in our unconscious. This debris can be washed away by the water of Spirit. Then we truly see!

It is interesting that all the healings of the blind were performed on men. That, too, has a deep meaning. As I have mentioned so often, androgyny, balance of the masculine and feminine within our psyche, is a requirement if we are to be totally healed. The masculine within each of us, both men and women, often blinds us to Truth of the Spirit. This Truth is feminine, this Truth is our Soul, this Truth is covered up by false beliefs. This Truth is often submerged in the reasoning, logical part of our left brain, the masculine. It needs the feminine, the Holy Spirit, to balance it and to bring wholeness. This, the Christ, the Feminine, awakens in us, but we must be open to It. We must believe.

After Jesus heard that the neighbors and the Pharisees were hassling the man over how he could have been healed when he was blind from birth and they had "cast him out" from among them,

Jesus found the man and asked him, "Do you believe in the Son of man?" The healed man asked who he was. Jesus answered, "You have seen him and it is he who speaks to you." "The man said, 'Lord, I believe' and he worshipped him." Now it is apparent that Jesus was speaking of the Christ that the blind man was now seeing. It was the result of that Son of man within Jesus by whom his healing came. It was that Divine Energy that healed. But we humans need something or somebody we can "see" to totally believe, and often worship the representative of that Loving Energy instead of worshipping the Energy.

Jesus ended his remarks with "For judgment (wisdom) I came into this world, that those who do not see may see, and that those who see may become blind." (John 9:39) What did he mean? He then says to the Pharisees (intellect) that when they say "we see" their guilt remains.

It is the nonacceptance of this deep Esoteric Truth on the Divine Energy, Wisdom, that makes us blind. We see from the intellectual viewpoint but are blind to the Spiritual Energy that is our Life. We can be healed, as the blind man, or we can deny the evidence of seeing as did the Pharisees. It is our choice.

In Verse 9, when the blind man heard his neighbors arguing about whether he was the blind beggar who had been healed, he said, "I AM the man." A testimony to I AM THAT I AM. He had come to his Self and knew who he was. That is how we are all healed from any dissonance in our Inner Being. We see. We are no longer blind.

Raising of Jairus' Daughter

Mark 5:21-24; 35-43

Our next example of the Christing of an individual by Jesus' touch or attention, is the account of the raising of Jairus' daughter. It is found in all three synoptic gospels.

The account is that Jesus had just given a sermon including references to the kingdom of God, also described was his quieting a storm, and healing a man possessed with a demon. He was surrounded by a great crowd. One of the rulers of the synagogue, Jairus, asked him to come and heal his daughter who was at the point of dying. He said that he believed that Jesus could heal her. Jesus went with him. On the way a woman who had had a flow of blood for twelve years was healed, and Jesus told her that her faith had made her well. This

117

wonderful account of the woman touching the hem of Jesus' garment and being healed by the aura of the Spirit that surrounded him, has been a classic in Christian teaching. (Mark 5:25-34)

As they went on their way, some of the ruler's servants came to tell Jairus and Jesus that the daughter had died, but Jesus said to the ruler, "Do not fear, only believe." When he arrived at the home he took Peter, James and John along with the parents into the room where the little girl lay. He had said there was no reason to weep for the little girl was not dead but sleeping. He took her by the hand and said, "*Talitha cu'mi*" which meant "little girl arise." And she got up and walked. She was twelve years old. He told them not to tell anyone and to feed her.

Let us go now to the deep meaning of this account which has been labeled an example of Jesus raising a little girl to life from seeming death.

At first, let us remove from our mind the traditional interpretation and be open and receptive to newness of Truth as it applies to our spiritual Journey. The girl was not "dead," she was asleep!

Jairus symbolizes "whom God enlightened." This gives us our clue. This is about Enlightenment. Jairus was not fully Enlightened, for he was the ruler of a synagogue. The synagogue symbolizes the religious thoughts that are focused on the outer law, focused on religious theology. These thoughts, however, were seeking life. The young daughter was his Holy Spirit that was asleep, seemingly dead, but was coming alive.

I wonder, could Jesus have been illustrating reincarnation when he raised Jairus' daughter as well as Lazarus. Remember that each time Jesus said each was not dead but asleep. In THE COSMIC FORCES OF MU by James Churchward, he writes that the ancients had no word corresponding with our word death. They called death "sleep." They saw what we call death as simply the sleeping of the soul until called upon to enter another house of clay in order to attain perfection of the soul over the flesh. This comes from Naacal writings.

This seems a viable explanation to me. The Resurrection of Jesus the Christ was a demonstration of the Light Body that surrounds and interpenetrates each physical body. This Light reincarnates in a physical body if there is need for further experience to attain perfection.

Talitha refers to soul energy within each of us (MBD), and it never dies. It is life, it is the Life Force, the Holy Spirit, and lives eternally.

Belief in the efficacy of the Christ moving within our seemingly dead consciousness requires faith and no fear. If we are afraid to allow the free flow of the Divine Energy it will be blocked. Fear is probably the greatest block. You see, the religious man Jairus did not depend on his outer religion for healing but turned to the Christ, the Healer. He let go of fear through his faith in Jesus Christ. He said, "Come and lay your hands on her, so that she may be well and live." (Verse 23) And he followed Jesus.

The healing Energy in the room where Talitha lay was very high as Jesus took with him Peter (faith), James (wisdom) and John (love) Also, the balance of the masculine and feminine, the mother and father, were in that room (state of consciousness) where the young feminine Energy was still and seemingly lifeless.

Jesus knew the Energy was Eternal and only needed the touch of his Life Energy to awaken It. He took her hand and commanded her to arise. He commanded the Kundalini Energy to arise, and it was so; and the masculine aspect gave glory to the feminine. Faith, Wisdom, and Love are needed for healing to the seeming death of the Spirit.

Then Enlightenment truly came to the religious thoughts that had been in control of the Seeker, of Jairus. When the Kundalini rises we Know that Spirit is our Guide and we let go of the power of outer religious theology. Jairus, the masculine, with potential for Enlightenment, was healed by the feminine and he had a flash of Enlightenment.

The girl was said to be twelve years old. This may symbolize a turning point; that is, twelve may symbolize a turning point in our life. Twelve is also a symbol of completion—completion of our Spiritual Journey. Enlightenment is symbolized by the number twelve. This is another indication that this account refers to the Inner Worship of the Spirit that seems to be dead but is only sleeping. It is never too late to allow dedication to the Christ to be awakened. Twelve may also refer to the twelve chakras that are En–light.

When she arose, Jesus told them to feed her. Attention to our Kundalini must continue. Feeding it means to be aware of it, prepare time to meditate, to go within to the Presence to guide our way, to quit misusing it. This is food for our Spirit.

Jesus again indicated that secrecy was necessary. Our most intense spiritual experiences should not be shared with the multitude, for talking about the Miracle will decrease the Energy and reduce the Light streaming into our consciousness.

"*Talitha cu'mi.*" Let us Know that this young feminine can arise throughout our body and brain and we are well, alive and can have mystical experiences as well as Enlightenment. We will feel that "touch" and It will arise.

A great deal of the teaching from Jesus as related to his healings took in the need for forgiveness as well as faith. He preached the gospel of the Kingdom before and after the healings, as if to demonstrate how one could be permanently healed from all separation from the Kingdom. It was not healing for healing's sake, but a demonstration of the power of the Lord which could be theirs if they turned within to the Kingdom of Heaven. Luke 5:17 says, "The power of the Lord was within him to heal." That power, he was teaching, lay within each of those in his company and within each human being.

We let Jesus touch us through the teachings of the Holy Scriptures. A deeper interpretation of these words and acts brings our Holy Spirit alive and we are truly Alive.

Healing Leprosy

Mark 1:40-45

Leprosy was a dread disease in those days, for it was painful, unsightly, and isolated the victim from all contact with others. It was contagious and incurable. It was an ugly disease showing itself in eruptive skin disorders of swellings, scabs and an eating away of the flesh. We have an account of Miriam, the sister of Moses, acquiring the dread disease and being healed by God through the intercession of Moses. (Numbers 12)

Jesus healed a number of cases of leprosy according to the accounts. We shall discuss only one.

In Mark 1:35 we read that after Jesus had healed Peter's mother-in-law, and many others, he went to a lonely place and prayed. We must all go apart from everyone and in our *temenos* (a sacred precinct) we meditate and pray. This brings up the ecstatic Energy and we are prepared for our service. Jesus had to recharge his body, brain, and consciousness to do his work.

Then he went with some of his disciples to Galilee, which symbolizes illumined thoughts that exalt the Christ, and preached in the synagogue and cast out demons from some who were there.

Beginning in Verse 40-45 we have the account of the leper. The leper came to him and declared his faith in Jesus' ability to heal.

Jesus, out of compassion and love, touched him and said, "I will; be clean." He told the man to go show himself to the priests and offer a contribution to them. And he asked him to tell no one of how he was healed.

When healed, in order to return to society, showing oneself to the priests and giving an offering was traditional.

There is a spiritual teacher, Heline, who suggests that leprosy may have been caused by the misuse of the Divine Energy in this lifetime or another lifetime. We know, of course, through Jesus' example that the Christ can heal any disease, whatever the cause. It is restoring that Divine Energy to its free flowing that heals. Faith in medicine and doctors can also awaken It to Its healing Journey.

Emma Curtis Hopkins says that Jesus healed the lepers by "feeling the sweet fires running along from the God Self of Himself, through the palms of His hands and the tips of His fingers as He sights with mystic energy the unseen Angel to wake joyous soundness where no waking seemed possible." (HIGH MYSTICISM, page 247)

It was that Divine Energy from the Christ that cured this seemingly incurable condition. The leper could not heal himself. This is true of us, usually, until we have reached a high state of consciousness by the activation of our Kundalini. We may need the teaching, the touch of another, for our Divine Energy to be awakened. But as we reach a higher level of awareness of our Kundalini Energy the body and mind remain filled with health.

The AIDS epidemic has some of the same characteristics as leprosy, with isolation from society and lack of healing. Let us all pray that a breakthrough in Spirit will come to these. Let us reach out in compassion and love to them and pass on some of our Vital Energy through caring for them. They can be healed and the medical world is doing its best to find a cure that will unblock that Divine Energy. This ailment is bringing many closer to their Inner Spirit.

Cancer is another fearsome disease that is being treated, sometimes satisfactorily by *materia medica*, but in many cases returns. Many cancer patients are turning to alternative methods of healing which include the touch of the Spirit through meditation, yoga, group therapy and devotion to their spiritual life. God is the healer. Our Divine Energy when released from blockage by fear can heal, but it takes great Faith.

So what is the esoteric teaching in this healing? The seeming incurable disease of negative living, of negative thinking, of living from our Shadow that covers our Good, of misuse of this Divine Energy, can be healed. We may need a teacher, a guru, a medical doctor, a spiritual healer. But more importantly we need to change our belief of isolation from the Spirit to reaching within to our Inner Spirit. This brings life even though the body may seem inert. There is no loss of this Vital Energy. We have it all. Our need is to recognize It, awaken It and unblock any obstruction to Its free flowing. Then the flow will heal. This flow is from another dimension which is Eternal Life.

There was no fear in this great Healer. He touched every kind of disease. His Energy protected Him from contamination. Our Christ Energy does the same.

There are those in the healing professions, psychologists, therapists, medical doctors who are realizing that eruptions on the skin are a sign that something deep within the unconscious has not been released and is causing the eruption. Like a volcano, when the pressure from our thoughts, our fears, our grieving erupt, physical signs follow. The I AM is being threatened. This recognition of the need for a cleansing and using dream analysis or other therapy is needed. Also medical help may be required.

The incurable can be cured. Could the answer lie in our activating our Divine Energy? It was Jesus' method.

Casting Out Demons

Luke 11:14-28

Let us turn now to a discussion of Jesus' "casting out" the demons from within men and women. We shall examine only one account of the healing of a man with an unclean spirit. According to one scholar there are seven accounts of Jesus' healings of people being freed of demon possession—five men, one boy and one girl. The one we shall discuss is in Luke 11:14-28.

As a background, belief in demons or devils was devised by the consciousness of the people of that time to explain aberrant behavior that they could not understand. Even today, specifically in India, spirit possession is believed in. Spiritual healers are said to be able to cast the demon out. Demonology was an attempt to explain the problem of evil which demanded a category of "superhuman" beings who have power over human beings. They were responsible for the moral and physical calamities. The inability to be rational lay at the door of an opposite force to Good, to God.

Now the devil, according to scripture, was conversant with God. (See the story of Job.) But neither the common people nor the priests in the synagogues had the power to heal the insane person. Sometimes this behavior was titled epilepsy. We have come a long way since that time in dealing with mental illness, but we are not "out-of-the-woods" yet.

Many ideas were brought forth as the reason for the demonic behavior in times past. Some believed, in Bible times, that the parents had sinned. Others believed the person was burdened with Karma from a former life and had to suffer in order to be free of that Karma in his future life. The Kahunas taught that insanity resulted when the Huna Force, the Kundalini, was divided by discarnate spirits who took over the body. This was spirit possession.

In Luke 11:14 we have an account of Jesus casting out a demon that had made the man dumb, unable to speak. Jesus was accused by the people of casting out demons by Beelzebub, the Devil. His answer, contained in Verse 17, says that a kingdom divided against itself will be laid waste. There is great teaching in that remark for us. If we are divided in our commitment to the Holy Spirit, we shall suffer.

Jesus said:

If it is by the finger of God that I cast out demons, then the kingdom of God has come upon you. (Verse 20)

In other words, if they accepted that the power of God had cast out the demon then they were in the kingdom of God consciousness.

He also pointed out that

"When a strong man, fully armed, guards his own palace (consciousness at a kingly level), his goods are in peace, but when one stronger than he assails him and overcomes him, he takes away his armor in which he trusted, and divides his spoil. He who is not with me (the Christ) is against me, and he who does not gather with me scatters."
(Verses 21-23) (Parentheses mine)

We must protect our Holy Spirit within our consciousness in order not to be scattered.

So any person who was possessed by a demon had no recourse but to live an abnormal life. There seemed to be no place to call home. They were a refuse on society thrown into nakedness, living among the tombs, being cast out. Jesus had compassion on these dregs of society! What love!

In that day there were those who believed that spirits of the dead had invaded the mind and body of the demoniac. These spirits were lonely and wanted a body to live in. So they invaded the conscious and unconscious of the demented one. These demon souls that invaded the body and mind of the living person had not taken care of their sins in a former lifetime.

Do you get the picture? These humans were lost, but Jesus restored them to their Self and to society. How? By touch, by Spirit-filled words, by love.

We remember that one of his greatest, most loyal followers was Mary Magdalene after he healed her. The Bible recounts in referring to her healing, that "from whom seven demons had gone out." (Luke 8:2) As an aside, although Mary Magdalene has been painted with the brush of a prostitute, there is no evidence in the Bible that she was one. She became the most loyal woman who followed Jesus and was the first to recognize him after his Resurrection.

It is interesting that the "casting out of demons" accounts state that the unclean spirits often called out to Jesus by name and recognized his power over them. In one Scripture two demoniacs called to him, "What have you to do with us, O Son of God? Have you come here to torment us before the time?" (Matthew 8:29)

This leads me to wonder: Were these demons of the same Energy as the Christ but was being misused by the individual who knew the Truth deep within his soul?

In each cleansing of the unclean spirit, Jesus rebuked the spirit, spoke to it with great power. He said that faith of the affected person or someone near to him was important for the healing. Prayer was also important.

Now why do I think that these healings are based on the passing of Jesus' Divine Energy to the affected one out of whom the unclean spirit came?

Because it is called a spirit. In Old Testament times, it was called a demon, but with Jesus it was called a spirit. In Mark 9:25 when he was healing a boy possessed by a "dumb spirit" he said,

> You dumb and deaf spirit, I command you, come out of him, and never enter him again.

He spoke to a spirit with a small "s." This was a negative spirit believed in by the boy and his father. It was to the affected personality that Jesus spoke, although it would appear he spoke to the un-

124

clean spirit. The affected person heard, and with the power of Jesus' *glance*, the strength of his *word* and his *feeling* of love, the healing happened. The man, boy or woman who was so afflicted "heard" at a deep level and the Power expunged the negative aspects of his/her personality.

We might say, in modern parlance, that the unconscious was affected by the Shadow of guilt, or fear, or lack of self-esteem, or abuses to the physical body or the psyche. The personality is "out of sync." It is the Shadow in the unconscious that needs to be released. Dream interpretation may be necessary. Dreams come from our inner Holy Spirit. Dreams are the "voice of God" speaking to us. All through the Bible we find instances of the great leaders and prophets being guided by their dreams. The Holy Spirit speaks to us while we sleep and interpreting those dreams will remove our Shadow.

With some of the healings of Jesus, the healed one followed Jesus and served him. Serving the Christ is necessary for the healing to be complete. After Jesus was accused of healing by Beelzebub, he told the parable of the man losing the unclean spirit, but the man went through waterless places and found no rest. Waterless means lack of Spirit. The man went back to his former house, consciousness, which he had put in order. But he goes out and brings in evil spirits and his last state was worse than his first. (Luke 11:24-26)

This is true of all healings. Jesus said, "Go and sin no more." That separation from the Spirit, or sin, must be left behind if the healing is to last.

Jesus, at One with the Christ, his Father, healed any and all who came to him with a sincere, humble desire to be healed. But faith and forgiveness were necessary. So it is for us.

So now, you may be wondering, how this fits into my Thesis. Let us look at some modern explanation for this deviance of personality. We have so much of this with our society today. We call it mental illness and provide the best care we know for them both physically and psychologically. But we are not healing and in some cases are looking again to shock treatment to heal depression when drugs and/or therapy have become ineffective.

Freud came forth with an explanation of insanity by blaming the sexual urges and the misuse of the libido energy as the reason for the deviancy. He opened to mankind the idea of the unconscious, which could hide many 'secrets' that needed to be made conscious. He did not take into consideration, however, the spiritual or superconscious part of the personality. Neither did he understand the libido as being anything else but a physical sexual force.

Carl Jung, conversant with this Freudian theory, took it further. He saw the libido as the sexual as well as the spiritual Force in each person. When this Energy was not blocked by the collective and personal unconscious, progress to individuation (Oneness) could occur. He did not preach any religion, but knew whereof he spoke from his own intellectual and intuitive knowing and experience with patients. His psychology is making inroads on the limitations of the Freudian theory and spreading rapidly in the healing of neurosis. For one who has lost complete touch with reality, psychosis, Jungian analysis may be less helpful.

According to June Singer, a follower of Jung, the modern day demons were called complexes by Jung. The complex seems to have originated in some experience in the life of the patient which made a deep and shocking impression, so painful that it could not be endured for long in consciousness. It was repressed. A complex is defined as a "constellations of psychic elements (ideas, opinions, convictions) that are grouped around emotionally sensitive areas." (See BOUNDARIES OF THE SOUL by June Singer, p. 37.)

Gopi Krishna has written and spoken on the activity of the Kundalini Energy. It was his belief that the insane, the genius, and the mystic were motivated by the rise of the Kundalini Energy to the brain and throughout the chakra system. He points out that the genius often ends his/her life in abject depression or suicide. The mystic accounts of the Dark Night of the Soul shows a temporary loss of the positive effects of the Kundalini. The insane person has either misused the Energy or has repressed it. The psychologists, for the most part, have not realized that the misuse of the Kundalini has caused this problem which could be alleviated if the healing Presence of the Energy could be aroused. In a speech I heard, Gopi Krishna's plea was that the psychologists study his theory. He maintained that many in our mental institutions could be healed and freed.

From some of his writings published in KUNDALINI FOR THE NEW AGE and edited by Gene Kieffer we learn in Chapter 7 that Gopi Krishna believed that the reason for insanity or psychosis is the prana (energy) acting in a "morbid way." This may be because the nervous system is not balanced, or heredity is not favorable, or the life is not well disciplined. These ideas remove all feelings of guilt from the one so burdened.

Gopi Krishna suggests that true psychology will begin when the research on Kundalini begins. It is not a science yet, he says because scientists do not recognize the nature of the life energy. Research needs to be done on the phenomenon of spiritual rebirth or mystical experience. "When pure, the bioenergy released by Kundalini causes the transports of ecstasy and the flow of genius, and when toxic, the nightmares of insanity." (page 115)

His theory is worth serious study and there are those who are doing research in this area of healing now.

Jesus never took credit for any of his work, any of his healings. Neither should we. His whole work was based on: "The Father and I are One." It is the God of the Universe that does the healing, not the person passing it on. Jesus taught on the spiritual rebirth and the need to be guided from the Spirit within. This is the mystics' way.

Psychotherapy, drugs, electric shock—all of these are used and some are successful. Why they are successful is not always agreed upon by the professionals. The healing often comes with no valid reason for it happening. If movement or the blocking of the Kundalini were taken into consideration, it would necessitate removing beliefs put forth by the Pharisees (the intellect) and turning to the Spirit, the Divine Energy within. How this Energy is to be activated is well documented in the religious literature of the East. Should we not study that and find an answer to the healing of the multitudes in our world who seem to be controlled by "demons"?

The people said that the demon was cast out by Beelzebub, the prince of demons. Others sought a sign from heaven from Jesus. Let us find the sign from heaven, the Divine Energy.

As Jesus finished his sermon a woman in the crowd shouted:

"Blessed is the womb that bore you, and the breasts that you sucked!" But he said, "Blessed rather are those who hear the word of God and keep it!"   (Luke 11:27, 28)

Perhaps our healing professionals are unable to heal by touch and by the Word, but recognition of their own Holy Spirit, dependence on their intuition to give them guidance when working with the one who has deviant behavior, and teaching the patient that the healing lies within themselves could bring nothing but good to this healing profession. Some are becoming aware of this. They are hearing the word of God and keeping it.

Jesus' Guidance to Healers

Matthew 10, Luke 10

For many spiritual healers today, accounts of Jesus' methods of healing are important. He not only healed but he instructed his disciples on *how* to heal. These directions that he gave them as he sent them out to heal should be studied deeply by those healers in our society today. This would be especially true of those who understand the healing power of the Kundalini Energy.

He sent out his twelve disciples at one point and "gave them authority over unclean spirits, to cast them out, and to heal every disease and infirmity." (Matthew 10) That authority I would suggest was his baptizing them with fire, the Holy Spirit, as John the Baptist predicted. (Matthew 3:11) He told them to go to the lost sheep of Israel, to bypass the Gentiles (thoughts that function through the senses) and the Samaritans (mixed thoughts, worldly and religious). They were to tell the "lost sheep" about the Kingdom of Heaven being there with them. They were to accept no pay. They were to bring peace.

They were to heal wherever they stayed and to turn away from those who would not receive them.

He said:

> Behold, I send you out as sheep in the midst of wolves; so be wise as
> serpents and innocent as doves. (Matthew 10:16)

Wise as serpents! Serpents symbolize wisdom, the Divine Feminine Energy. Also dove is symbolic of that innocent Holy Spirit.

He pointed out that if they were taken before governors and kings to be charged, that they were not to be anxious for "it is not you who speak, but the Spirit of your Father speaking through you." (Verse 20) *There* is his most important directive. That is the Intuitive faculty coming from the Holy Spirit on which the healer must depend. That intuition will be the Guide as to how to heal. He taught them to heal by this method. When the twelve returned they were ecstatic and reported great success.

In Luke 10 we have the account of Jesus sending out Seventy disciples into the field. He gave them many instructions. "Heal the sick and say to them, 'The kingdom of God has come near to you.'" (Verse 9) The Seventy returned with joy and reported their success. Do I need to say that the Kingdom of Heaven is that Ecstatic State that results from moving the Kundalini, the Holy Spirit, from the lower chakras to the Throne at the top of the head. Jesus praised the disciples for their success. He said,

> For I tell you that many prophets and kings desired to see what you see and did not see it, and to hear what you hear, and did not hear it.
> (Luke 10:24)

Prophets and kings could refer to the medical doctor, the psychologist, the therapist and to all mental healers who do not "see or hear" the Truth which is that healing of diverse diseases depends on releasing the blocked Holy Energy through Faith, Repentance and the Touch of the Spirit.

As we read and study these accounts we are reminded of our important responsibility to serve when we have been baptized by the Holy Spirit. To do this our own healing Energy must be at a high level to receive instructions as to what we are to do and what means we are to use to effect the cure. It is the consciousness of the Holy Spirit within that does the work. Jesus always gave credit to "the Father within." It is not the healer that effects the cure. The healer is the instrument through which the Holy Spirit flows. Also, one must have a deep realization and belief that the healing will take place. This is the teaching of Jesus Christ. Faith as KNOW-ING is needed.

The West is opening up to Truth that the East has known forever. The Kundalini Energy, active in each human being, is teaching and healing. Longevity will give us each more years to recognize that Christ, that Holy Spirit, and we then can follow It in creative activities, in service to our fellow beings, and in demonstrating the glories of its effect on us.

The opportunities are here. Ecstasy, Kingdom of Heaven, is here and now. We can experience It.

Thus we end a very short account of the healings performed by Jesus the Christ and his instructions to his followers. His teachings and examples have affected the healing profession, both *materia medica* and spiritual healers for thousands of years. We are beginning to realize the efficacy of his methods as we understand the flow of that Eternal Energy within our body, emotions, and thoughts. Alternative medical practices are based on this knowledge as well as knowledge of effective methods for cures that have come to the West from the East. I believe that Jesus knew these methods either by intuition or by having visited the East as many researchers believe.

Illnesses can be alleviated by the releasing of this Divine Energy, the "Spirit of your Father" speaking through us. Healers and those in need of healing should pay attention. In Matthew 10:26, 27 Jesus, in giving directions to his disciples, said,

> So have no fear of them; for nothing is covered that will not be revealed, or hidden that will not be known. What I tell you in the dark, utter in the light; and what you hear whispered, proclaim upon the housetops. (RSV)

This I have attempted to do. The secret is out. Rest and abide in It.

Since Light has been such an important aspect of our teaching, let us now study It.

Chapter XVI

THE TEACHING OF JESUS ON LIGHT

Jesus spoke often of Light. The recorders of Jesus' words made it an important aspect of his teaching. Light has intrigued the mind of humankind forever. Light of the Sun has been worshipped for aeons. These worshipers were religious groups that believed the light of the sun was so important for life that they worshipped it and sacrificed animals and human beings to it. They believed they were keeping life aglow in the world by so doing.

And of course we have the statement from Genesis 1:3, 4, which is:

> Then God said, "Let there be light"; and there was light. And God saw that the light was good; and God separated the light from the darkness.

That is the Creation.

To define Light as such seems impossible from an intellectual level. We are still in the "dark" as to what It really is, but from the spiritual level we have many teachings on It.

I would like to quote some teachings from Jesus on Light. Matthew 5:14, 16:

> You are the light of the world. A city set on a hill cannot be hid. Let your light so shine before men, that they may see your good works and give glory to your Father who is in heaven.

Jesus was giving his Sermon on the Mount and said to the listeners, "You are the light of the world."

In other words, each of us is Light and our Light lights the world. This is the Light that abides within us. This is the One. This is the Holy Spirit, the Kundalini. It manifests when our intellect, our ego, gets out of the way.

Let your Light shine in good works so that others who see them may give glory to the Father who is in heaven. The Father is that Holy Spirit of Jesus. Heaven is our consciousness of the Oneness which we uncover little by little. Jesus was speaking to each of us, for our Light shines whatever our conscious awareness of It may be. John 8:12:

> Again Jesus spoke to them, saying, "I am the light of the world; he who follows me will not walk in darkness, but will have the light of life."

I AM is the Light of the world. I AM is that One that abides in each of us and in all. The I AM is the Holy Spirit, the spark of the Godhead. "You are the light." When we follow that I AM all will be Light in our outer as well as our Inner Life. We are all drawn to the Light like moths to a lamp. Our lamp is that consciousness which gives Light when we provide it with oil.
And another, John 12:36:

> While you have the light, believe in the light, that you may become sons (daughters) of light."   (Parenthesis mine)

Now we always have the Light but we may be unconscious of It. Then we walk in darkness, and stumble. We may fall into ditches, into pits of anger and pain, but still the Light is present and through a small glimmer It calls us on. When we believe in that Light we are moved from the darkness and we are conscious that we are children of Light, that we are children of the Incomprehensible One. And Light is our consciousness.

But this does not define the Light does it? Well, that is impossible. There are no words that can adequately define Light. It just Is. Someone said, "Is is Is." That is Light. Jesus said Light was life. If so, then wherever the Light is there is life. There can be no death, for our Soul is Light and "Is is Is . . . "

Carl Jung compares Light to the libido, which he defines as sexual as well as spiritual energy, being One. He said,

> "The libido expresses itself in images of sun, light, fire, sex, fertility and growth."   (SYMBOLS OF TRANSFORMATION, page 221)

We have all had the Dark Night of the Soul when there seemed to be no light. That darkness is lifted when we have an increase in consciousness of the Light for consciousness is Light. Indeed consciousness is that Divine Being we have called God, a limiting term for that Primary Energy, and is beyond definition or naming.

That Presence is who you and I are. That Presence is all. That Presence is the Light of the world. You are the Light of the world. You are that Presence. To be conscious of That is your spiritual task.

Notwithstanding, Light has been defined as Truth, Wisdom, Sophia, Intelligence, Holy Spirit, Inspiration, Intuition. We often say when solving a problem, "The light dawned." What a profound statement. Indeed, Light (truth) dawned upon our conscious awareness. This Truth lies waiting for our attention.

In one of Jesus' most profound quotations on Light we have:

> The eye is the lamp of the body. So if your eye is sound, your whole body will be full of light; but if your eye is not sound, your whole body will be full of darkness. If then the light in you is darkness, how great is the darkness. (Matthew 6:22, 23)

We notice first that "eye" not "eyes" is spoken of. The Third Eye is *that* Eye. The Third Eye at the Sixth Chakra in the forehead is where the Inner Light glows and can be "seen" when one has followed the Path of meditation, contemplation and devotion to spiritual consciousness. That Light can be "seen" by the deeply advanced Seeker or Yogi. That Light can also be seen in the aura of an advanced Seeker. All is Light. But if our Eye is not open then darkness will be throughout our body and affairs, and "how great is that darkness!"

The Third Eye symbolizes wisdom, the feminine aspect of the Godhead. Moving the feminine Energy to the Seventh Chakra, brings together the Shakti and Shiva and Oneness is experienced.

The Third Eye is filled with Light and all darkness has disappeared. Jesus said that at that point the whole body is full of Light. This is the Transfiguration of darkness to the Light, the changing of the physical body to that Exalted State of Pure Light.

Remember our Ten Virgins? Each had a lamp and that lamp needed oil to continue to shed light. The "eye" is that lamp and must be fed with the Divine Energy, the oil. The foolish virgins had darkness, for their lamps were not fed by attention. We must give attention to our lamp, to our Third Eye Chakra, in order to have Light for our Journey.

We could also interpret this "eye" as the Spiritual "I."

Joel Goldsmith, a mystic who has led many on their Journey, wrote a book entitled THE MYSTICAL I, in which he refers to this "I" as God and says that "I" stands at the door of our consciousness and knocks. It is up to us whether we open our door and experience the Light of the "I."

133

This Light is the Light of each of us. This Light, Divine Energy, can transform the cells of our physical body so Light and health and Joy will prevail. We are aware of this as we read the Transfiguration account. Jesus' physical body was filled with Light and he appeared to Peter, James and John who had to be at an Enlightened level of consciousness to see this Light Body as well as the Ethereal bodies of Moses and Elijah who had long ago left the earth. (Matthew 17:1-8)

The Enlightening experience of Awareness of Light is a high spiritual experience and changes the consciousness and life of the observer. Maurice Bucke reports on enlightening experiences of many men in COSMIC CONSCIOUSNESS. These visions came as a result of light, not without, but from within. These men also, many times, had the Inner Voice experience.

Eckhart taught that an excess of Light in the Soul flows out into the external body and it becomes full of brightness. Light, he says, is intuition, and gleams from within, and we know how to direct our mind to express it either in speech, writing, art, music, science, or any creative activity.

Emma Curtis Hopkins in HIGH MYSTICISM, wrote that Intuition is identified with Light.

The Source of Light, she wrote, we have called God, and when the recipient has the experience of Light they Know God. Their mind and body are transfigured by the Light. This Light is our Inner Spirit showing forth.

But for all that, Light remains a mystery, so Yogananda says. The devoted of every age have testified to this existence as God and is "seen" in a flame as well as indescribable Light. The Taoist has taught of the Oneness of dark and light. The practice of *Tai Chi* makes the dark and light One. This Oneness is expressed in the creative activities of calligraphy, painting, music, gardening and the act of love.

I have had more than one Light experience and the Voice coming to my conscious awareness. This changed my life, howbeit unconsciously. After the first experience it took me years of being in the Dark to understand It, but It was with me and is with everyone, for It is the Presence showing forth to our physical and spiritual senses.

The Transfiguration of Jesus on the high mountain is our greatest demonstration of being In The Light, Enlightened.

Your Kundalini Energy is Light. Let it shine!!

Chapter XVII

THE TRANSFIGURATION OF JESUS

Matthew 17:1-8; Mark 9:2-10; Luke 9:28-36; John 1:1-5, 9, 11-13, 16

Let us first define transfiguration from the mental set: To change in outward form or semblance; to transform. Transfiguration as a Christian term refers to the change in Jesus' physical form to a Light form as witnessed by three of his disciples, Peter, James and John.

This Transfiguration of Jesus with accounts in Matthew, Mark, and Luke have some slight differences in the description but are very much the same. These translations bring in the teaching on Light which has interlaced this entire book, and we have given it special treatment in Chapter XVI.

For some, transfiguration is a figment of imagination; that is, that human eyes could see a physical body become a Light body. But mystics throughout the ages have attested to the Reality that the physical body is just a shell filled with Light. Light Beings can be experienced through visions, dreams, trance and imagination. Some testify that the "touch" of the Being is felt at a deep level, both physically and spiritually. Jesus said, "While you have the light, believe in the light, that you may become sons of light." (John 12:36) He also said in the same chapter, verse 46: "I have come as light into the world, that whoever believes in me may not remain in darkness." His Christ was the Light. Our Christ is the Light. We believe in that light; we have Faith, Knowing and then Being in the Light.

In I John 1:5 we read: " . . . God is light and in him is no darkness at all." And Revelation 21:23 refers to a description of our completion in the Kingdom of Heaven. "And the city has no need of sun or moon to shine upon it, for the glory of God is its light, and its lamp is the Lamb." The Lamb is the Christ. Yet the body can be lost in darkness if no outer light shines upon it. We cannot see it with physical eyes, but spiritual eyes see through the darkness.

Jesus admonished us to let our light shine. He said that we are the light of the world and not to hide it under a bushel, but allow it to light the world.

In Alice Bailey's book FROM BETHLEHEM TO CALVARY she sees the Light experience as one of the Initiations we must all go through. Development of spiritual understanding increases the Light and develops an inner radiance. Then we can say, "I am the Light of the world." Each of us has the potential for this experience.

Enlightenment is really self-explanatory. It is the consciousness filled with Light, the physical body changed to its natural Light body. The body then is called by various religions the solar body, the diamond body, the adamantine *Nirvana* body, the light body, the rainbow body, the resurrection body (Christian). It is deathless and composed of a Spiritual Substance.

As we have discussed time after time, the aura, the crown, the nimbus around the body and head all occur because of the Light, the Divine Energy which has impregnated the physical cells and is shining around them and through them.

There are those who teach that Light shows us that the Cosmos is alive, entirely spiritual, that there is no death. *All* on earth have a Light body. When we have an experience of the super-normal Light it is a Cosmic experience, beyond definition and still we try.

Although the account of the Transfiguration is contained in the three Gospels, there are those scholars who teach that the first chapter of John refers to Transfiguration. Not specifically that of Jesus, but Transfiguration which could relate to each of us. John was of course one of the Apostles who witnessed the Transfiguration of Jesus and thus would be aware of this Divine Example.

References to Light might suggest this. So let us study those verses in John 1 which deal specifically with Light, but is called Word.

In Verses 1, 2:

> In the beginning was the Word, and the Word was with God, and the Word was God. He was in the beginning with God;

As explained previously Sophia, Wisdom, testified that she was in the beginning and was the Creatrix of all. She was the Word referred to in John 1, which would come to the world in the body of Jesus. Therefore, let us read these scriptures from the feminine mode.

> . . . all things were made through him (her), and without him (her) was not anything made that was made. In him (her) was life, and the life was the light of men. The light shines in the darkness and darkness has not overcome it. (Verses 3-5)

This Word, this Light, is the Christ. It was Christ that came into the world. It is Christ that comes into the world at the birth of each human being. This Christ is our Holy Spirit.

Remember Jesus referred to the Light in the Eye overcoming the darkness? He said that if our Third Eye is filled with Light our whole body will be filled with Light. That is Transfiguration.

John 1:9:

> The true light that enlightens every man (and woman) was coming into the world. (She) was in the world and the world was made through (her), yet the world knew (her) not.

It is the Kundalini, the Chi, the Life Force, the Divine Energy that is spoken of.

John 1:11, 12:

> He (she) came to his (her) own home, and his (her) people received him (her) not. But to all who received him (her) who believed in his (her) name, he (she) gave power to become children of God;

Each of us is "her people" and we may not be conscious of her, the Light. If we are, we will have great power and be true children of God.

> Verse 13: who were born, not of blood nor of the will of the flesh nor of the will of man, but of God.

And Verse 16:

> And from his (her) fullness we all have received grace upon grace.

From the fullness of our Holy Spirit we receive grace upon grace.

The Word, the Spirit, takes on flesh and we are born to proceed on our Journey. The Light that is hidden will be revealed and a Transfiguration or Transformation of our life will occur.

Let us go now to the actual account of the Transfiguration. Since the accounts vary somewhat, I shall choose from each that which seems appropriate to my illustration that this Transfiguration, while Jesus was yet in human form, is symbolic of Truth. We shall quote Mark 9:2-4:

> And after six days Jesus took with him Peter and James and John, and led them up a high mountain apart by themselves; and he was transfigured before them, and his garments became glistening, intensely white, as no fuller on earth could bleach them. And there appeared to them Elijah with Moses; and they were talking to Jesus.

Six days may refer to the six chakras that were overflowing with Light within Jesus. He felt this high ecstatic awareness of the Holy Spirit and knew he must go apart from the world to a place of high consciousness (mountain). He had Faith (Peter), Wisdom (James) and Love (John) functioning in his high state of consciousness. He turned within and awaited the experience that was to transform his awareness of who he was. Matthew Fox says that at his Transfiguration, Jesus became aware of who he was—the Cosmic Christ. (See THE COMING OF THE COSMIC CHRIST by Matthew Fox.)

The brightness of countenance and body attest to a high level of consciousness. We are all aware, consciously or unconsciously when we are in the Presence of a highly evolved man or woman. We may not "see" the Light but we can feel It. We are raised to a higher level.

In Luke 9:32, the scripture records that Peter and those with him had gone to sleep and when they awakened they "saw his glory and the two men with him." The two men, Moses and Elijah, were also in Light bodies.

When we are in a state of half-sleep and half-awake, we are in another dimension and often see figures that are no less real than when we are wide awake. This refers to the fact that the three disciples were in an altered state when they saw the three Light figures. Seeing a Light Being requires one to be out of the mental into the spiritual or psychic. Our "eye" is open and our soul becomes aware of Light as it truly is in the living flesh body, and also the spirit body of those who have left the physical body through death.

Moses symbolizes the Law, Elijah symbolizes fulfillment of the Law, and Jesus symbolizes the I AM in the present with the Law on Love which he emphasized. Moses and Elijah had their own experiences of Transformation on a high mountain; thus they came together with Jesus, the one who was bringing a new dispensation to the world. They all three had had their temptations while in the flesh and had overcome them.

I should like to emphasize that we each go through those levels of consciousness. We each have our temptations, our dark times, before we rise to the Light. We each have our crucifixion and resurrection. Finally our ascension comes when we are Enlightened. Each of these—Moses, Elijah and Jesus exemplify these three stages.

Peter, even though at a high level of awareness, allowed fear to interrupt the vision. He suggested to Jesus that booths should be built for each one of them to keep them on the earth. (Matthew 17:4) This idea engendered by the intellect out of fear made the vision vanish and only Jesus remained in his physical/light body.

A cloud then covered them. The cloud has been interpreted as a vehicle for the Shekinah, the feminine aspect of God. The cloud led the wandering Israelites in the wilderness by day, and the cloud covered the mountain when Moses was receiving the Ten Commandments and other laws for the Israelites. This Shekinah spoke to Jesus and the three. This voice, an Inner Voice, speaks to us also.

The voice spoke, "This is my beloved Son, with whom I am well pleased, listen to him." (Matthew 17:5) This voice had been heard at Jesus' Baptism. However, *this* message was different. It contained "Listen to him." Jesus was ready to do his major work.

The disciples then fell on their faces "and were filled with awe." When they got up only Jesus was there. He asked them not to tell anyone about the experience "until the Son of man should have risen from the dead." (Mark 9:9) The Son of man rises from the dead within us when we have an experience of Enlightenment.

"What is Enlightenment?" we might ask. Even though we try to understand, it has been a mystery for thousands of years, and still is, for it is an experience beyond cognition.

Enlightenment, when final, takes one out of the space/time creation.

The raising of consciousness to awareness of the Divine brings a consciousness filled with Light, the physical body changed to its natural Light body.

I like Lex Hixon's definition from his COMING HOME, page xi: "Enlightenment is the awakening of primal harmony or, in another mystical language, to our rootedness in the Divine." To know that I AM, this sacred Presence, is Enlightenment, he says. All spiritual practice is preparing us to be able to remain continuously in that Presence.

When we deeply Realize that we are already En-Light, the One, we are Enlightened. Thomas Keating says that at Jesus' Enlightenment, the divine Source of Jesus' human personality poured out through every pore of his body in the form of Light. (THE MYSTERY OF CHRIST, page 43)

Now Light is the Christ, your own personal Guide and Savior. Light is Truth. Light is KNOWING, not just believing. We are En-Light when we experience that Resplendent Creative One, the Shekinah, the Sophia, the Kundalini, the Holy Spirit fully. That Light changes our life little by little as we let It shine.

Here are some ideas for you if you are interested in bringing forth your Light:

- Believe It is within your consciousness.
- Seek It through meditation.
- Trust It—have Faith in It.
- Listen to inner promptings for Guidance and follow—open your mind.
- Accept the Gift of the Presence and give thanks.
- Use your judgment to separate Truth from error. Learn to recognize Truth.
- Feel the glory, the power, the Ecstasy from the Christ within.
- Be at One—KNOW, LISTEN, FOLLOW.
- Have Ecstatic rejoicing—this is Enlightenment.
- Keep your experiences secret. Do not waste the Energy by revealing the "High" to others.
- Go out and serve the Christ through serving your fellow-persons.
- Rejoice in the Holy Spirit, the feminine Energy, within your body and consciousness.

There were other Enlightening experiences for Jesus—many of which were not recorded, I suspect. His experiences are for our teaching. We do not get stuck in awe over our experiences but come down from the mountain, tell no one, and take the Light forth to heal others. Immediately after Peter, James, John and Jesus came down from the mountain Jesus healed a young boy possessed by a demon. His Light was used in service to others. This must we do also.

Thus ends a very short account of the Virtue of Jesus the Christ as he spoke and acted from the Christ within. His Crucifixion, Resurrection and Ascension were all Light experiences also and were witnessed by many besides Peter, James and John. All that he did, we can do also. The Christ within is our Holy Spirit and great and marvelous are the results when we see the Truth of Who we are. We shall discuss the Enlightened Jesus further when we study Paul's experiences with the risen Lord as well as that Lord's appearance to John as he recorded the Book of Revelation.

At his Ascension, the Christ said: "You shall receive power when the Holy Spirit has come upon you . . . and you shall be my witnesses to the end of the earth" and "he was lifted up, and a cloud took him out of their sight." (Acts 1:6-8)

The feminine Energy, the Shekinah, of the cloud took the Christ's Light Body and scattered it throughout the Universe.

And So It Is!!

Chapter XVIII

THE RESURRECTION: WHAT IT MEANS TO US

The last two chapters on Light and Transfiguration are an introduction to the account of the Christ's Resurrection as reported in all four Gospels, to wit: Matthew 28; Mark 16; Luke 24; John 20.

Each account is preceded by a description of the trial and crucifixion of Jesus and his body laid in a tomb, a sepulchre, a rock-hewn tomb and the entrance closed with a heavy rock which was rolled into the opening. The morning of the Third Day some of his women followers (notice it is the feminine) came to anoint his body with spices and herbs. But they found the tomb empty and were told by an angel to go tell his disciples and Peter (Mark 16:7) that Jesus of Nazareth would meet them in Galilee (Energy of life. MBD) This infers that the disciples would have high Energy or Light flowing in order to see him. The women were afraid and ran away. The feminine is often our deterrent to realization of our Resurrection. Another account gives us the meeting of Mary Magdalene (the power of love, devotion and service) with the Risen Christ. Other accounts, some of which seem in opposition to each other, tell of his being seen and heard by the disciples and many other witnesses. On these accounts of Jesus Christ's Resurrection the teachings of traditional Christianity hang.

As an aside I should like to say that in many other religious accounts we have the founder being resurrected from death. One of the major ones was Osiris of the Egyptian religion which teaching preceded the Jews living in Egypt and then they carried much of that teaching in their sojourn in the Holy Land. Moses was their teacher and their Leader. He was trained in the Egyptian religion. This does not discount the Resurrection of the Christ but only adds credence to It.

143

Other religious leaders who had overcome death are Tammuz, Zoroaster, Aesculapius, Hercules, Baldur, Mithra. Many would discount these accounts calling them legends or myths. But the followers of the religion acknowledged their Resurrection as Truth, as do the Christians in believing in the Resurrection of the Christ.

For many of us, this account of the Christ's Resurrection is pure Truth, for we have experienced the "seeing" and the "hearing" from that Christ as we went on our Journey. Many times this happened when we were at the deepest low point in our physical/spiritual life. Jesus Christ has appeared to innumerable witnesses throughout the centuries. This, seeing Jesus Christ as a Light body, has been the awakening agent to start the individual on their Spiritual Journey. This experience is never forgotten and has motivated the seer to take up the Purpose for which each was born. We know more about this from the Christian viewpoint but according to religious historians a like experience of seeing their leaders in the Light Body came to those whose belief was centered in god-like Teachers and Mystics. So we accept that the Christ in the Light Body has come to many.

The historical account of Jesus' Resurrection by the transforming of his physical body to Pure Light has led to the tenets of many Christian denominations. Different interpretations of the Resurrection has also caused many wars and cruelties to other human beings.

This belief in life, in death, in overcoming seeming death is in the collective unconscious. Overcoming the fear of death has been a human assignment and belief in the Resurrection, belief that we each have this potential to rise from seeming death, has and does make life more bearable for many. There are those scholars who see the Resurrection of the body, of the Spirit, as the paramount theme of the New Testament and for Charles Fillmore it is and was the all-embracing subject in the entire Bible. (ATOM SMASHING POWER OF MIND, page 116) No wonder the Christ's Resurrection has been such an important theme in the Christian religion.

There is much written today on Near Death Experiences when the individual's life is turned around and each continues the physical/spiritual life filled with the Light of understanding. All of those who tell of their experience report that they have lost the fear of death. Many are met by a shining Light figure whom they relate to as Jesus Christ or a loved one. The traditional fear of death is overcome.

I had a Near Death Experience in 1984 and can attest to the fact that I have no fear of death and my Purpose became paramount in my life after that Experience. That Purpose was to carry the message of the Christ, of the Light within, to thousands of readers of my books. The Light Figure of Jesus Christ had come to me many years previous to that Near Death Experience, and I had been cared for through those years. That Light Figure of the Christ is more Truth than Truth to me.

As I have explained so many times—the Light is the same as the Kundalini Energy. When the body and consciousness are completely transformed from the physical and the mental to Pure Spirit of the Light Body, it is called Enlightenment. That is a Resurrection. We have few accounts of Resurrection happening in our present day, but since Jesus taught that we could do what he had done and more, I must assume that it is possible for each of us also.

Let us go now to the esoteric interpretation of the Resurrection. Let us see that this Divine Beauty permeates our body, soul and mind, and let us relate the Resurrection to our own Journey. But first I should like to quote a scripture, Revelation 1:12-18 which describes the Vision of the Christ experienced by John the Disciple.

> Then I turned to see the voice that was speaking to me, and on turning I saw seven golden lampstands, and in the midst of the lampstands one like a son of man, clothed with a long robe and with a golden girdle around his breast; his head and his hair were white as white wool, white as snow; his eyes were like a flame of fire, his feet were like burnished bronze, refined as in a furnace, and his voice was like the sound of many waters; in his right hand he held seven stars, from his mouth issued a sharp two-edged sword, and his face was like the sun shining in full strength. When I saw him, I fell at his feet as though dead. But he laid his right hand upon me, saying, "Fear not, I am the first and the last, and the living one; I died, and behold I am alive forevermore, and I have the keys of Death and Hades."

This was Jesus Christ who came to John to reveal the deepest mysteries of our individual and humankind's Journey back to the New Jerusalem. It is that Journey that the Resurrection is about. The first Resurrection is letting go of the intellectual choice of the physical over the spiritual, which means rising from the dead. (See Revelation 20:5, 6) Later John tells us in Revelation how this Resurrection opens the Way for our final awareness in the Kingdom of Heaven, the New Jerusalem.

We can interpret the tomb as our imprisonment in our human personality. Resurrection is letting go of the belief that we are merely human. That is needed for our first Resurrection. We are in a tomb of earth, hard rock consciousness when we believe that we are merely human. We are imprisoned behind a huge stone and only an angel of the Lord can roll it away. Then we accept that we are a Divine Being of great value to God's Purpose and begin to reveal our hidden Beauty. Resurrection from the collective unconscious belief in death is our task. Alice Bailey says in FROM BETHLEHEM TO CALVARY, page 252: A true resurrection is not the rise of the dead from their tombs but the passage from the death of self-absorption to the life of unselfish love, . . . to the light of universal spirit . . . to truth . . . to the liberty of the eternal. (Edited)

Eternal life has always been a human goal. Some explain this by suggesting that the Soul has left the Godhead to express on planet earth and is always striving to return to that Source and have Eternal Life. Jesus Christ often used Eternal Life and Kingdom of Heaven interchangeably.

This Kundalini, this Holy Spirit, is then free and we may become Ascended Masters to appear in the visions and the lives of innumerable human beings to help them overcome their earth consciousness and go forward in Divine Consciousness.

In John 11:25 we read (Jesus was speaking to the woman at the well):

> Jesus said to her, "I am the resurrection and the life; he who believes in me, though he die, yet shall he live, and whoever lives and believes in me shall never die. Do you believe this?"

Such an important question for us also.

Here Jesus states: I AM is the resurrection and the life. I AM, we have established is the same as the Christ, as the Light, as the Kundalini Energy. That is the Resurrection. That is Eternal Life. To Know *that* is our goal. That is why we must die to physical consciousness, usually on the cross of materiality, and be buried in the rock of physicality. But we all have the potential to rise from the grave as a pure Light being and go forth teaching Love and Resurrection.

Resurrection is then the elevation of spiritual consciousness emancipated from the intellectual prison. This may happen to us many times from the intellect to the Spirit, before we make the final transition into Pure Light, pure awareness of Who we really are. Jesus Christ's demonstration brought hope to humankind that the grave was not the end but that the Spirit would live on. This has helped overcome that human propensity—fear of death. When we accept our Light–ness then we are ready to carry the love message to others by service. Thus did our Wayshower, Jesus the Christ. When the stone of materiality is rolled away we are resurrected by the Christ power that is within our consciousness. It is Grace that carries us Upward.

Barbara Marx Hubbard in her book THE REVELATION: OUR CRISIS IS A BIRTH writes that we are at a turning point in human consciousness and that Resurrection, raising of our consciousness of Oneness with God, is a given. She writes:

> The intensity of that love, the power of connectedness is the key to the resurrection, now known as the transformation.   (page 61)

She says the Christ's Resurrection was a future forecast of what each of us could do in transforming from Homo sapiens (creature) to Homo universalis (co-creator). But loving God above all else and our neighbor as ourself is required. And so we are back to Love, that expression of our Divine Energy as we seek our own Resurrection.

Let us each know that the Resurrection is possible and more important, probable, for you and me. Let us Know that the Christs's example has lifted us higher and we are invigorated by the account of that Resurrection given in the Gospels. Let us

> "Go into all the world and proclaim the good news to the whole creation."   (Mark 16:15 NRSV)

This GOOD NEWS is our own Resurrection!!

Thomas Troward says in THE DORE LECTURES: "The *principle* of the Resurrection is the realization by man of his individualization of the Spirit and his recognition of the fact that, since the Spirit is always the same Spirit, it becomes the Alpha (beginning) of a new creation from his own center of being." (page 67) Thus our true Resurrection takes place on a new day in consciousness when our attention is on the Spirit, when we realize that we are Individualization of the Spirit. That is our Resurrection. That is Pure Light.

Chapter XIX

THE ACTS OF THE HOLY SPIRIT

The Book of Acts has been the guide, the foundation of much of the teachings and beliefs of the Christian church. It contains a description of the apostles being baptized by the Holy Spirit, their establishing the first churches based on their understanding of Jesus' teachings, accounts of their healings, their difficulties in setting up rules for the first churches and the accounts of Paul's missionary journeys and his teachings.

The teachings of Paul as recorded in the Book of Acts by Luke, as well as in other Books that Paul is said to have written, are very important to traditional Christians. Much of these teachings have been interpreted literally. Jesus' teachings are also important although the interpretations of them have caused much dissension within the Christian church as well as within other religious groups.

Paul's writings have been analyzed, discussed, rejected and declared Truth for millenniums. Although he had no personal physical experience with Jesus, the visitations by Jesus to Paul through visions for his guidance provided him with courage, healings, and strength to establish many churches far and wide. The Holy Spirit led him.

On this guidance of the Holy Spirit much of the Acts of the disciples rested. They all acclaimed Its place in their work. The Holy Spirit, the Kundalini, the Chi, Wisdom brought about that which Jesus predicted for his apostles when at his Ascension he said:

> But you shall receive power when the Holy Spirit has come upon you; and you shall be my witnesses in Jerusalem and in all of Judea and Samaria and to the end of the earth.   (Acts 1:8)[1]

These were his final directions to his apostles.

---

1. I refer you to Chapter XII for a discussion of Acts 1 and 2.

And so it was and is for it is that Holy Spirit that sends each of us into Jerusalem (peace); Judea (praising God); Samaria (intellect). The Holy Spirit, the Kundalini, brings guidance for our thoughts and clears them, converts them to praising God from which comes Eternal Peace.

The Holy Spirit is referred to 38 times in the Book of Acts, and Spirit (the same as Holy Spirit) 13 times. To Her is given the credit for healings, for guidance, for protection, for raising the dead, for carrying the gospel (good news) to the ends of the then known world.

The Book of Acts was written by Luke, the physician, who traveled with Paul on some of his missionary journeys. He also wrote the Gospel of Luke. Acts was written about 70 A.D. It emphasizes taking the Truth to all.

In discussing Paul's teaching, I have chosen to focus on his visions, for visions are directly related to the Divine movement of the Kundalini, of the Holy Spirit, to bring the recipient an enlightened experience. Paul's missionary journeys opened many to the Holy Spirit also.

The account of his conversion from persecuting the followers of the Way to his leading many to the Christ is a myth that teaches us.

Paul was journeying to Damascus (warring thoughts) to arrest some Christians, which he had been doing for some time. His first vision of Jesus was recorded in Acts 9:3-6:

> Now as he journeyed he approached Damascus, and suddenly a light from heaven flashed about him. And he fell to the ground and heard a voice saying to him, "Saul, Saul, why do you persecute me?" And he said, "Who are you Lord?" And he said, "I am Jesus whom you are persecuting; but rise and enter the city and you will be told what you are to do."

The men with him heard the Voice but saw no one. When Paul arose from the ground he was blind and after he was led to Damascus he would not see for three days until a man named Ananias, a follower of the Way, had a vision of Jesus and was told to go heal Paul. Paul was prepared for Ananias' visit as he had had a vision of him. Ananias said to Paul:

> The Lord Jesus who appeared to you on the road by which you came, has sent me that you may regain your sight and be filled with the Holy Spirit. (Acts 9:17)

He laid his hands on Paul and his sight was healed by the Holy Spirit and he was baptized by It. Paul was reborn, inspired, filled with power and courage and eventually became that great missionary spreading Jesus' teaching far and wide.

In one account of this Vision on the road to Damascus, Paul says that Jesus said to him:

> "It hurts you to kick against the goads." (Acts 26:14b)

Those goads are with us also. They are our thoughts that open to the Inner Spirit but we reject them. And we are hurt until we turn the goad into centeredness on that Holy Spirit, the Christ. Paul called this Holy Spirit the Christ.

When Paul took his message to the Jews he was reviled and so he declared, "From now on I will go to the Gentiles." The Gentiles (heathens) were classified as non-Jews and rejected by the Jews.

The Lord appeared to Paul one night in a Vision and told him not to be afraid to go on his Mission. He told him:

> I am with you, and no man shall attack you to harm you; for I have many people in this city." (Acts 18:10)

This Vision came to support him in his difficult work of trying to convince the Jews that Jesus was the Messiah, the Christ. His Vision and Voice experience from his Holy Spirit gave him the support that he needed and he turned to the Gentiles.

In Acts 23, Paul was in deep trouble:

> The following night the Lord stood by him and said, "Take courage, for as you have testified about me at Jerusalem, so you must bear witness also at Rome." (Verse 11)

And thus he did.

Paul could not avoid following these Visions of Jesus which appeared to him. When we have a Vision and/or Voice experience it changes our life. We are never the same. We may receive our Commission or we may not "hear" it until later in life. But we will answer "yes" or die. We are chosen and must follow the Inner Guidance of our Kundalini, our Holy Spirit, and go forward knowing the Christ as our Guide.

According to Luke's account, Paul established many centers of worship. He performed healings. He baptized with the Holy Spirit. His Holy Spirit guided him in his writings and the Christian church has given him honor and a place of Sainthood in its organization.

Paul's teachings seem confused at times and in our modern day do not fit the level of race consciousness to which we have evolved.

But his demonstration of the Holy Spirit as spoken of in his writings teach us all.

Some of his greatest teaching is on our immortality. Let us quote I Corinthians 15:51-55:

> Lo, I tell you a mystery. We shall not all sleep, but we shall be changed, in a moment, in the twinkling of an eye, at the last trumpet. For the trumpet will sound and the dead will be raised imperishable, and we shall be changed. For this perishable nature must put on the imperishable, and this mortal nature must put on immorality. When the perishable puts on the imperishable, and the mortal puts on immortality, then shall come to pass the saying that is written: "Death is swallowed up in victory." "Oh death, where is thy victory? O death, where is thy sting?"

Now this has often been interpreted by Christianity as referring to death of the physical body and our spiritual body rising into heaven. I think this has a deeper esoteric meaning.

Jesus taught time after time that the Kingdom of Heaven, of God, was within. In fact that was one of his major, if not the major, teaching. That is why he came to earth, this Jesus Christ, to teach us that we do not have to wait for death to our physical body to bring us to the Celestial Level of ecstasy, peace, love, joy, for it lies within us. It is at hand. That is the meaning of Verse 55. There is no sting in death to our humanness. There is only victory.

It is devotion to that Inner Christ which much of the New Testament refers to. It is letting that Victorious Holy Spirit be all that we are. We are that celestial body. The physical or terrestrial body, made of earth (all of our food comes from a combination of heaven and earth) gives us the opportunity to express, to live from, to serve from our physical attributes. But all of this is for the Spirit, for God. This is for the Son of God. All of this Jesus Christ taught repeatedly. He gave us the Guidance. Although humankind has waited 2000 years to understand, a few mystics have understood it always. Meanwhile the Christian world's interpretation was laid on Paul's teaching and taught for consciousness of that day and indeed now. Physical death has been *writ large* in the minds of many.

We are in a New Day, a New Age. We are awakening to the true, true meaning, the symbolic meaning of Paul's teaching and although he wrote for the pilgrims of his day, much of his teaching fits our Journey now.

In I Corinthians 13 Paul writes his great discourse on Love. Love is God. We are Love. We are the Holy Spirit which is Love. And he says:

> "If I speak with the tongues of men and of angels but have not love, I am a noisy gong or a clanging cymbal." (Verse 1)

What a humble confession after all the words he had spoken. And he wrote: "Love never ends."

The Divine Energy is Life, Light, Love. It is the Holy Spirit directly from the Godhead. It never is dead. All life depends on it and Paul knew this. We Seekers KNOW this when we turn within to that Holy One. Visions shall be ours. Guidance is ours. We listen and follow as did Paul.

The apostles and disciples were also busy carrying our their Mission. Let us go to them now.

The disciples and the apostles of Jesus Christ were on fire with the Holy Spirit after the day of Pentecost and went forth to carry out Jesus' Commission for them. They accepted their Purpose for living.

The Holy Spirit, the Divine Energy, or the Kundalini, is spoken of often in the carrying out of their Mission—to convert, to baptize, to heal, to guide the people. This Holy Spirit activated, changed the lives of those who were in the early church. Later that Holy Spirit as the Inner Free Spirit was not available to the individual according to church doctrine. The activation of It could only come from the leaders, the teachers, or the authorities of the church or synagogue. Fear was engendered in members of the church if they reported the activation of the Energy within themselves, and so the deep secret was lost.

The Eastern religions have taught us the Secret. the Kabalists also knew it, but it was not taught to the general members of the synagogue. It has been the deepest secret in our Bible. Since meditation has become a common practice for millions in the West we are discovering this Secret of the Inner Spirit that knows All and Guides us to our Enlightenment.

In Acts 2:38 Peter is speaking to the multitude after the disciples at Pentecost had been visited by the Holy Spirit and spoke in other tongues. When the multitude gathered, Peter gave his first sermon.

> Repent, and be baptized every one of you in the name of Jesus Christ for the forgiveness of your sins; and you shall receive the gift of the Holy Spirit.

They heard and "there were added that day about 3000 souls." (Verse 41) That was the beginning of the early church.

Repenting or letting go of the darkness in our conscious and unconscious mind, being baptized in the name of Christ which is our Holy Spirit, will bring us the gift of the activation of the Kundalini within.

Repentance may require our attention to our dreams as the Holy Spirit speaks to us through our dreams and visions of the Light. The Holy Spirit is our Self and is forever moving us higher and higher as we give attention to it through meditation.

Peter often spoke from the Holy Spirit. In Acts 3 Peter, filled with the Holy Spirit, healed a cripple and spoke in defense of his action.

In Acts 5:15 Peter's shadow healed as the sick were carried out into the street and laid on pallets so that his shadow might fall upon them, and they were healed. Peter's "shadow" was his Light aura, the Holy Spirit, the Kundalini activated and glowing all around his physical body.

In Acts 8:17 we have the account of many Samaritans who received the word of God but had not been baptized by the Holy Spirit. Peter (faith) and John (love) went to them.

> Then they laid their hands on them and they received the Holy Spirit.

One last example of the activation of the Holy Spirit: Peter had given a sermon. He pointed out that God anointed Jesus of Nazareth with the Holy Spirit and with power, and he healed the sick, for God was with him. (Acts 10) After they heard the sermon, "The Holy Spirit fell on all who heard the word." (Verse 44) The Gentiles received It.

God gives us the Holy Spirit. The Kundalini is a spark of the Divine. It is through Her Grace that we become conscious of It. God has a plan for our life. Guidance from our Inner Knowing will help us fulfill it. It is not the guru. The guru is the instrument used by God to awaken us. God gives us our baptism by the Holy Spirit.

The disciples were sent out by the Holy Spirit. The disciples were filled with Joy and the Holy Spirit. Joy is our treasure and comes from within under the auspices of the Holy Spirit.

The disciples healed by this Divine Energy. Peter healed Aeneas who had been paralyzed for eight years. He raised Tabitha or Dorcas from seeming death.

Tabitha had served her community well and the mourners in gratitude stood with the garments in their hands that she had made. She had given too much of her Energy in service. We must not use too much of our Energy in service to others, either. We must give our spiritual life much attention through the Silence, through being separated from others, through Holy Work.

There is more, so much more scripture referring to the Holy Spirit. The Holy Spirit led the disciples as they established the first congregations. They listened and followed to the best of their ability. They may have made mistakes but so do we if we are not completely free of ego. Each must decide in what direction they are to take their own spiritual life. No one has all the answers for another.

I should like to quote a few more verses from the Book of Acts referring to the Holy Spirit.

Acts 10:38:

> . . . how God anointed Jesus of Nazareth with the Holy Spirit and with power; how he went out doing good and healing all that were oppressed by the devil, for God was with him.

Acts 13:52:

> And the disciples were filled with joy and the Holy Spirit.

And one from the Book of Romans and I Corinthians:
Romans 14:17, 18:

> For the kingdom of God does not mean food, and drink but righteousness and peace and joy in the Holy Spirit; he who thus serves Christ is acceptable to God and approved by men.

I Corinthians 6:19:

> Do you not know that your body is a temple of the Holy Spirit within you, which you have from God? . . .

Testimony to the power and activity of the Holy Spirit is throughout these great Books. What more testimony do we need to be convinced that the Holy Spirit resides in our heavenly temple?

The Holy Spirit active in these disciples gave them the strength, courage, love, and power to convince people to follow Jesus Christ. Many of the disciples were sacrificed in the name of their teaching. We are sacrificing our own Energy oftentimes, not in serving others, but in fear of our own welfare, in attachment to others or to our own self-will. Sacrifice for others may be our Mission, but sacrificing our own Divine Energy, our feminine Wisdom, for physical ex-

155

citement and accumulation of things will not bring us true Joy. It is giving this Kundalini in service to our own Christing and the needs of others that will bring us real happiness. It lies within. The disciples were filled with Joy and with the Holy Spirit when they "shook off the dust from their feet." (Acts 13:51) (Paul and Barnabas were persecuted by the Jews and thus left the district where they had been teaching.) Sometimes it is necessary for us to "shake off the dust from our feet" to become detached from those who have chosen a different Way. When we do, our love is still with them and though saddened we go on our Way rejoicing with the Holy Spirit.

We find much emphasis on the Divine Energy throughout the remaining books of the New Testament which we have not discussed. In the King James Bible the Holy Spirit is called the Holy Ghost. One more reference to It:

II Peter 1:21:

> No prophecy ever came by the impulse of man, but men moved by the Holy Spirit spoke from God.

That underscores our Thesis. Prophecy is based on intuitive Knowing and it comes from the Holy Spirit, from God. When our lives are guided by that Spirit we are becoming Enlightened. We are creative. We are fully alive.

The scriptures written on the teachings of Jesus Christ are important guidance for our own Journey, but we must realize that the Holy Spirit, the Kundalini Energy, is within us and *There* is our Guidance.

This account of the teachings found in the Gospels, Acts, books written by Paul and others, has brought us from the Law of the Old Testament to a realization of the newness of the Word of the Christ. We are in another age and it is proven each day by the outer events of our world; by the scientific breakthroughs; and the movement in consciousness of the Spirit that is taking place in many Seekers. The worldwide communication network of TV, radio and other media has carried these new but old Truths to many. However, wars still go on, sickness continues—spiritual, physical and psychological—and we sometimes hear nothing but negativities about the human race. But we know, from our own experiences, that pain and hurt often precede a Breakthrough in consciousness. I believe we are being prepared for that Breakthrough. We are being prepared and when we accept, then humanity will give the Spirit, that Holy Spirit, first place in their life and affairs, healing will occur.

Many believe that we are in the End Times. Yes, we are. We are moving toward the world that the Book of Revelation describes, especially in the last two chapters. The last chapter describes the throne of God's Truth which teaches that the Truth is that we are in "a new heaven and a new earth" right now and we will see, with John, the "holy city." And we are Home.

Chapter XX

THE BOOK OF REVELATION

Revelation 2, 3

This wonderful book is one of the most important in the entire Bible and I have seen it as a demonstration of my Thesis par excellence. Finding the Kingdom of Heaven consciousness through the clearing of blocks in the body, mind and emotions by the activity of the Kundalini is its theme. This survey of the spiritual Journey experience for every Seeker, and the end result, gives all of us guidance for our Journey.

As a background I must share with you my experience with this great book.

My Spiritual Journey, at least consciously, started at the death of my only son in Vietnam in 1966. Or I should amend that to say it started as a result of a precognitive dream about his death. That dream convinced me that there was a Power over which I had no conscious understanding that prepared me for the shock of the visit by the army person to apprise me of his death. As a result of that great gift and grief, I started my Search for my own spiritual identity and my spiritual Haven.

Meditation, reading, reading, reading, opening of Truth in my unconscious a step at a time was the result. I attended some seminars but worked largely alone. I was employed as a high school counselor at the time and had no family responsibilities. It is too lengthy an account to go into detail, but I finally found a metaphysical church group that taught what I was beginning to believe. The support of that group invigorated my Search.

After some years I began writing poetry that came to me "out of the blue." In 1978 looking forward to retirement and after a year of dream analysis by a Jungian analyst, and at the same time studying

Jung Psychology, I was deep in meditation and heard from my Inner Self, "Write an interpretation of the Book of Revelation." I was overwhelmed since I had never read it, thinking it was beyond understanding. I argued with my Inner Self but then acquiesced, and the project was started. That launched me on my Purpose: writing spiritual, non-literal interpretations of the Bible.

As I delved into the Book of Revelation I realized it was an account that fit Western as well as Eastern religious philosophy. I saw it was not the horrendous end-of-the-world account, but a guide for our Spiritual Journey with ups and downs, but final success when one reached the new heaven and new earth, when there would be no tears, no death, no mourning, no crying or pain. (See Revelation 21.)

Much of the interpretation came through inspiration from my intuitive Knowing, much came from the study I had made of world religions, and much came from my intellectual understanding. It was published in 1981 and has had a second printing and a very popular acceptance.

It is from this book, REVELATION FOR A NEW AGE, that I shall discuss my Theme, i.e., that the movement of the Divine Energy lifts us to the height of awareness of Who we are.

As an introduction to prepare you, I have used metaphorical interpretation throughout the book as well as many references to Hindu and other religious teachings, and Jung psychology. Also basic to the interpretation is the Christian understanding of the teaching of Jesus Christ as interpreted from a liberal viewpoint.

John, the Apostle of Jesus Christ, is accepted by many scholars as the recorder. 70 to 95 A.D. has been given as the possible dates for its recording.

Revelation 1:9-11 and 17-19 tell of a Light and Voice vision that John had of Jesus Christ and the receiving of guidance to write what he "heard." The teaching was to be addressed to the seven churches at Ephesus, Smyrna, Pergamum, Thyatira, Sardis, Philadelphia and Laodicea. These were locations of early churches.

In Revelation 2 and 3 we have direct quotes from John's Vision of Jesus Christ. The rest of the book contains a description of the teachings that were given to John by Jesus. I shall deal mainly with these chapters. They demonstrate the Journey for each of us as our Kundalini Energy opens the seven chakras represented by the seven churches.

During our Journey we each have some cleansing to do. This cleansing comes to our intellect (thoughts), our emotions (feelings), to our physical body and our outer experiences. These cleansings unblock the Way for the Spirit to take us to Oneness.

The seven churches are described from their positive as well as negative characteristics. We shall read the messages to them as applying to our own Journey. Charles Fillmore and Paramahansa Yogananda would agree.

We have explained the route of the Kundalini Energy as moving up the spine and cleansing physically as well as spiritually the seven chakra centers. The messages to the churches tell us how. So let us begin.

The Church at Smyrna I have designated as representing the First Chakra. (Revelation 2:8-11) I have named this one Faith. Faith is a prerequisite for our Journey. As the Kundalini is activated the awakening occurs in the First Chakra. The Journey is begun. Faith is activated in various ways. Paul says that Faith comes by hearing, and hearing by the Word of God. The exact quote from the New Revised Standard version is "So faith comes from what is heard, and what is heard comes through the word of Christ." (Romans 10:17) What is "heard," whether from the Bible, a sermon, a teaching, or perhaps a Vision/Voice experience touches our Inner Knowing, the Christ, which we have designated as the same as the Holy Spirit, the Kundalini.

There are glitches in the church at Smyrna; there are tribulations and belief in poverty, according to the Voice. For our personal Journey these can come from our belief in the poverty of our Spirit, in what others say of us, or by our own misgivings. But the Voice says that we are rich and should have no fear. Starting the Journey is the greatest step, for it will lead to detachment from worldly possessions and needs and perhaps detachment emotionally from people who do not understand or follow the same Way. Unconsciously we will know that we are being urged on by the Inner Christ, however.

In Revelation 2:12-17 we read of the message to the church at Pergamum. This I have placed at Chakra Two.

The message to the church at Pergamum is complimentary at first in that they kept the name of the Christ and did not deny faith. But they have Satan dwelling among them. Verse 14 recites some negatives:

> But I have a few things against you: you have some there who hold the teaching of Balaam (mental sense plane), who taught Balak to put a stumbling block before the sons of Israel (spiritual thoughts) that they might eat food sacrificed to idols and practice immorality.
>
> (Some Bibles use fornication, adultery.)

161

The Second Chakra is located in the area of the sex organs. I have named this chakra "creative power." We all have the possibility of being creative as we activate our Faith. Indeed it is part of our Path, but we may get off the Path if our Energy is locked or adulterated at the Second Chakra. We may have raised our consciousness to the Fourth Chakra of love or beyond, but we may slip back; and through sexual immorality the Energy may be blocked. Misuse of the creative Energy is often a great temptation for the beginning Seeker. Indeed, many accounts in Eastern religions indicate this as a great temptation for the advanced Seeker also. The church is warned about the use of the Energy in this way. This sexual desire must be balanced with love and wisdom. The Voice tells John that if this is overcome "I will give some of the hidden manna, and I will give a white stone, and on the white stone is written a new name that no one knows except the one who receives it." (Revelation 2:17b)

Manna is the Divine Energy, the Kundalini. The white stone is consciousness purified. The new name is I AM. When the misuse of the Energy is overcome the reward is great and further expansion is possible.

When we are creative in our work, in art, music, poetry or any artistic endeavor, we are at our happiest, for we are listening to that Divine Energy and are following our Purpose. Finding our Purpose will usually include being creative. Creativity is God expressing through us. Allowing that Divine Energy to move up to the higher chakras will allow us to express something that needs to be passed on to other citizens of the world. It is our Joy.

The Third Chakra at the solar plexus I have named Intellect, which is power. The church symbolizing this is Ephesus. (Revelation 2:1-7)

The intellect can also block our Way when we consider it our power. It can be misused by our ego and move us away from our spiritual intuitive Knowing, and hearing Guidance from the Christ.

The church at Ephesus is accused of abandoning the first love (Faith) and they must repent and do the works that Faith directs them to. When they have overcome this block they will "eat of the tree of life that is in the Paradise of God." (Revelation 2:7) The tree of life is the spine up which the Kundalini flows to bring our consciousness to the Kingdom of Heaven, the Paradise.

Overcoming dependence on our intellect to give us the good life may be our most difficult overcoming. The higher the intellectual quotient the more power we often have in the phenomenal world. It can bring us wealth, status and power, but it may not bring us Paradise. Finally we repent of our ignorance, deflate the ego, and turn to that "word of the Christ." We use our intellect to express and live that Word, but the Intuitive Knowing guides the Intellect.

Having Faith and overcoming lust and egocentricity, we move to the Fourth Chakra designated as the Love level of our Journey. Here we study the message given to the church at Philadelphia. (Revelation 3:7-13) This chakra, at the heart, is filled with feelings of love for God, our neighbor, and ourself. Most of us reach this level of feeling now and then, on and off, throughout our life but sometimes misinterpret the feeling, either through our thinking or through our misuse of the sexual energy we believe is expressing love. Sometimes we go through great pain before we learn this lesson, but love is a bright star that we all long for. This love is called the "key of David." The Christ is teaching that the "holy one" has those keys. The "holy one" is the Speaker, the Christ.

The Voice says that those who have love have an open door to the city of God, but Satan (material thoughts) may interfere. There will be trials to our expressing that love, but they will be overcome, and a new name, I AM, will be given when Love is experienced freely. The I AM is pure God consciousness.

Verse 12:

> He who conquers, I will make him a pillar in the temple of my God; never shall he go out of it, and I will write on him the name of my God, the new Jerusalem which comes down from my God out of heaven, and my own new name.

In Verse 11 he mentions that "no one may seize your crown." When we are practicing pure love we have the Crown of Life, our Seventh Chakra, which cannot be taken away.

Now that the door of Love is opened we shall advance on our Spiritual Journey. Love neutralizes the negatives of our past and we go forward to a higher dimension of consciousness. The opened Fourth Chakra is the turning point.

The Fifth Chakra at the throat center I have named Worship. The church chosen is Thyatira (Revelation 2:18-29) Worship in many religious ceremonies consists of using the vocal chords to make a sound of worship to the God they believe in. Chanting, singing, reading scripture aloud, spoken testimony of belief, praying—all make use of the sound of worship and lift the Seeker higher.

The congregation is complimented at first. Love, faith, service and patient endurance mark their progress, but there is a misuse of the Spiritual Energy in tolerance of Jezebel (of the world and earthly pleasure). (Verse 20-23) When one "backslides" great distress follows, as the higher or deeper we go the more is expected of us. Using the fifth chakra power for fulfilling ambition on the physical level will stop our progress. The misuse of the Energy at this center is called adultery. Adultery can be committed in many different ways. We adulterate our bodies by drinking and eating what is unhealthy. We adulterate our emotions by negative feelings, those we recognize and those we push down into our unconscious. We adulterate our thoughts of the world as they are filled with desires that are not based on Spirit.

How can we heal this "glitch" in our Journey? By keeping away from the misuse of this Power in worshipping worldly endeavors. "Keeping my word until the end" is the admonishment.

Repentance is needed. Facing our weaknesses at this level of our Journey is sometimes most painful. Spiritual egotism may get in the way. We have come a long way in this lifetime and previous lifetimes. We feel we almost "have made it." And then this block of the outer world, separation from Spirit, raises its head. Sometimes we go down in defeat at this point. Words spoken are not uplifting and positive. The Word of our Christ is not on our lips. We adulterate this great Power of the Spirit. At this point the Seeker may choose death of the physical body and then return again in another lifetime to overcome this weakness. Sometimes the Soul born into another physical body will start the Journey all over again, or perhaps at a higher level. Whatever we have gained in our former lives is never lost. It comes forth when we are ready.

So what are the keys to further advancement on our Path? Here are a few: desire, commitment, positive use of personal will, meditation and prayer, and living an exemplary life based on Truth. Listening and expressing the Word of Christ from within our consciousness will bring Truth. But blocks must be removed to the thinking and speaking of the Truth every day. Our human condition may block it. Meditation on the Inner Self, listening and following is Truth and will turn our worship to praise and thanksgiving.

We are coming now to the Sixth Chakra, the church at Sardis. (Revelation 3:1-6) The sixth chakra is designated as Wisdom by religions of the East. It is the Third Eye which the Egyptian religion, as well as others, described as the ultimate while in a physical body.

We have interpreted Wisdom as the feminine Energy, the Kundalini which has reached its home in the Sixth Chakra. The church at Sardis represents Wisdom. True Wisdom is next to Enlightenment.

Even at this level we are warned that we still have overcomings. The Speaker says that the Seeker seems to be alive but is dead. He warns them to hold fast to what they have experienced.

What is Wisdom? A question that the human intellect cannot fathom. Humankind often believes that the ultimate in Wisdom has been reached but there is more—much more. It is alive, not dead. Our level of Wisdom evolves as our consciousness evolves. It is that Divine Energy, the Kundalini, a spark of the Divine.

The Speaker promises to those who conquer, to those who overcome their sleepy condition, that they will have robes of white (light bodies) and their name will be in the book of life. If they do not awaken, the results will be like a thief taking away what they have.

We must continue on, we must listen, we must repent of any errors and we must reverse our intellect from the negative to love of the positive. This allows us to ascend to the Kingdom of God and have the Ecstasy we all long for.

Wisdom is intuition, is pure Knowing, is the Word of the Christ. According to the Bhagavad Gita, "When Wisdom is thine, Arjuna, never more shall thou be in confusion; for thou shalt see all things in thy heart, and thou shalt see thy heart in Me." The Lord Krishna was speaking.

"Yet, Wisdom," according to Jesus, "is vindicated by *her* deeds." (Matthew 11:19) Our deeds show forth our level of Wisdom.

Being at one with Creative Intelligence, is our Goal, and Wisdom leads us to that final step. The Kundalini Energy is unblocked and the Seventh Chakra is opened.

The message to the Church at Laodicea (Revelation 3:14-22) gives us our final guidance. Verse 14:

> And to the angel of the church in Laodicea write: "The words of the Amen, the faithful and true witness, the origin of God's creation. . . ."

The words of the Amen are the same as the Words of the Aum. Yogananda says the Aum is the voice of the Divine Energy, the Holy Spirit, the invisible life force that upholds all creation. (AUTOBIOGRAPHY OF A YOGI, page 370n) According to this scripture, the Amen is the origin of God's creation, and so the Angel of our Holy Spirit is speaking to us at the Seventh Chakra.

We are ready to have the Enlightenment. It may be a brief experience but when the Chakra is filled with Light, our life will never be the same. That experience is for Eternity, and although we may meet many challenges and temptations we will never forget that brief instant of Enlightenment and It will forever call us on. We are in the Kingdom of Heaven.

The Seventh Chakra is called the Thousand Petaled Lotus, the Crown. The spray of light that fills and surrounds this Chakra of the Aspirant is visible to those who see the aura.

But perfection is not reached yet. The Speaker says that when we arrive there we are a faithful and true witness, but sometimes we misunderstand what this level of awareness is about. He says we are lukewarm.

Once having reached this high state of consciousness we may become lukewarm in our spiritual trek. If we drop down, our second condition is worse than our first, for we have seen, have experienced, the Goal and may find it difficult to stay at that level in the physical world. Lukewarm is a rather peaceful condition and seems to be the *nirvana* state. But the Speaker says, "You cannot stop now. Either get on with it or get off." We will find our whole life has changed after this Enlightening Experience. We cannot just drift. We are counseled in Verse 18 "to buy from me gold refined by fire, so that you may be rich; and white robes to clothe you and to keep the shame of your nakedness from being seen; and salve to anoint your eyes so that you may see." (NRSV)

Gold is the pure metal that cannot be destroyed, and symbolizes the perfection of the Holy Spirit, the Pure Spirit that is One with the All That Is. The purity of Spirit is always there. Our task is to uncover it.

Fire, the Sacred Flame, burns away the dross that surrounds that gold. This may be painful but we sometimes need pain if we are to clear away the dross. Self-assessment to uncover that dross in our unconscious can come through meditation, contemplation, dream analysis, active imagination (conversations with our Inner Self) or with the help of a therapist who is spiritually centered. Thank God, psychologists are beginning to practice the teachings of Jung, which puts spiritual Oneness as the apex of our Search for Wholeness.

Verse 21 promises a place on the throne to one who conquers. There we shall remain at One. We have reached our Kingdom of Heaven consciousness for all time.

I have covered in this chapter a minute part of THE BOOK OF REVELATION. However, these teachings are repeated over and over in the rest of the book in symbolic language. A description of our individual Journey follows these two Chapters. In writing on Revelation the positive side of this Journey is emphasized, although there are dark times.

The last two chapters, 21 and 22, are most important. To close this Book I should like to quote from them, for they give a description of the end result of our long Journey to the Kingdom or Dominion of Heaven Consciousness. This is taken from THE NEW TESTAMENT AND PSALMS

> Then I saw a new heaven and a new earth; for the first heaven and the first earth had passed away, and the sea was no more. And I saw the holy city, the new Jerusalem, coming down out of heaven from God, prepared as a bride and bridegroom adorned for each other. And I heard a loud voice from the throne saying,
>
> "See the home of God is among mortals. God will dwell with them; they will be God's peoples, and God will indeed be with them; God will wipe every tear from their eyes. Death will be no more; mourning and crying and pain will be no more, for the first things have passed away." (Revelation 21:1–4)
>
> The Spirit and the one bethrothed say, "Come". And let everyone who hears say, "Come". And let everyone who is thirsty come. Let anyone who wishes take the water of life as a gift. (Revelation 22:17)

And I say AMEN!

Chapter XXI

FINIS

This is really not the end, the *finis* but the beginning of our realization of the magnificence of the Holy Spirit, the Kundalini, the Divine Wisdom in our life. Writing this book has lifted my consciousness to new spiritual heights, as I hope reading and contemplating it will do for you.

"The grace of the Lord Jesus be with all, Amen." (Revelation 22:21) We have had our journey. Along the way we may have been puzzled at some of the explanation of how this Divine Energy expresses as our very Life. But as we have looked deeply into the "secret," esoteric meaning, our consciousness of Truth has been enhanced and our understanding of the Biblical accounts has reached a new depth. Archaic terms have been interpreted for the modern reader, the modern Seeker.

Bringing together Eastern and Western philosophy makes us One. We are not separated from our Eastern brothers and sisters. Our Western Way has been our talisman and the Eastern Way is the same teaching in different expressions. The Lord Jesus Christ lived and taught in an Eastern culture. His teaching has reached out to all humankind whether from North, South, East or West.

From Matthew to Revelation we have demonstrated the teaching of the activity of the Serpent Energy hidden for ages in the pages of the Judeo/Christian Bible. This Energy is bringing about great changes in government, religion, health practices, science, art, literature and all forms of the public media. We are in a "new era." When understood and accepted as Truth for our individual lives, great progress toward what Christianity calls the Kingdom of Heaven will be made. It can be experienced here on earth in your physical as well as spiritual Being. It is recognition of our Oneness with ALL THAT IS.

My hope and prayer for you as the reader, as the Seeker for One-ness, is that some chapter, some statement, some esoteric Truth contained in this interpretation of the Great Book, the New Testament of the Bible, will strike a deep note within your consciousness and you will go forth to find your own Path. The Way is open—follow It. Amen, *Aum, Hum, Amin, Om, "The Word."*

And So It Is!!

Addendum

KUNDALINI, THE DIVINE ENERGY

In Eastern religious teaching it is through the raising of the feminine Energy by meditation, chanting of mantras, various yoga exercises of stretching and relaxing the body, concentration or contemplation, or through Shaktipat by a guru that the Consciousness is raised and the body is purified. (This list is not all inclusive.) Thus the body cells vibrate at a higher level and the body, the physical, is changed to pure Light. The yoga undertaken is called Hatha Yoga by the Hindus.

How is this done?

The teaching is that this Energy rises up the spine and the central channel, the Sushumna, through two channels called Ida and Pingala. As this energy ascends it affects the whirls of energy called chakras. Their number is variously given as 6, 7, 9, 12 or more, depending on the particular teaching, but in Hinduism six is the common number with the crown chakra the seventh. These chakras are at the location of the endocrine glands in the physical body. The chakras are in the ethereal body which has the same form as the physical. (See JOYS WAY by Brugh Joy for his account of locating these energy centers.)

As the Energy is aroused and moves up the spine, consciously or unconsciously, the chakras are en–lightened and the nerves/nadis of the subtle body are filled with energy. This results, many times, in the seeker hearing different sounds in the body, seeing light within or outside of the body, and many other reactions. When the Kundalini is functioning at a high level there can be the sound of music, of bees humming and other distinctive sounds coming from within. Above all, the aspirant will have creative ideas come forth which must be, or should be, recorded in art, music, writing or expressed in other creative ways. And Ecstasy arises!

Now why would one be interested in this exercise? Well, of course, in the West few are; but in those who use various yogic methods or have Shaktipat (a touching of the seeker by an advanced Yogi whose Energy is active), or chant, or meditate or move the body in certain rhythmic ways, the Energy is raised. To be deeply immersed in spiritual expansion by activating the Kundalini brings very high ecstatic experiences. These Initiates are healthier, freer, more intelligent, more intuitive, more loving, more self-directed, creative, more at peace than the common run of humanity. This is often experienced as the Kingdom of Heaven consciousness that the Christ spoke of so often.

St. Paul spoke of this process in his writing. Jesus the Christ also spoke of it in parables, in symbolic language, and demonstrated it in the Resurrection in his Light body as well as his healings and raising some from the "dead."

In Tantra Yoga this Divine Energy is raised through a man and woman coming together for spiritual purposes. (This will be a very brief description. If you are interested you can find books describing the process.) The inner Fire which normally would be used for sexual pleasure and generation is the procreative fluids of the body which through this Tantra process are retained in the body and not spilled. The retention of these fluids filled with Energy allows it to be moved up the spine to the highest chakra and great ecstasy is experienced. This is considered a spiritual exercise devoted to their God.

In the Taoist secret teaching we have exercises of breathing and circulating the Energy. (See THE SECRET OF THE GOLDEN FLOWER, translated by Richard Wilhelm.) The Golden Flower is the same as the thousand petaled lotus, so called by the Hindus. However, this book is based on the Taoist/Buddhist teaching of China. This is the crown chakra fully opened. The goal is to translate the body and consciousness to a higher vibration and this culminates in Enlightenment.

St. John of the Cross speaks eloquently of this Energy in his book, LIVING FLAME OF LOVE:

> From this it follows that the delight which the soul receives in the rapture of love communicated by the fire of the light of these lamps is wondrous, and boundless, being as vast as that of many lamps, each of which burns in love . . . and thus all of them become one light and one fire, and each of them becomes one light and one fire. (page 208)

So these lamps of fire are living waters of the spirit like those that came upon the Apostles, which, though they were lamps of fire, were also pure and clear water as the prophet Ezekiel called them when he prophesied the coming of the Holy Spirit, saying: "I will pour out upon you, saith God, clean water, and will put My spirit in the midst of you."
                                                                        (page 211)

And from Gopi Krishna:

This mechanism, known as Kundalini, is the real cause of all genuine spiritual and psychic phenomena, the biological basis of evolution and development of personality, the secret origin of all esoteric and occult doctrines, the master key to the unsolved mystery of creation, the inexhaustible source of philosophy, art and science and the fountainhead of all religious faiths, past, present and future.
      (KUNDALINI, THE EVOLUTIONARY ENERGY IN MAN, page 176)

One of the clues to this teaching on the Kundalini lies in the symbol of the serpent. In the Western teaching on the serpent we have always been encouraged to be fearful of it. It was given a negative connotation in the account of Adam and Eve in the Garden of Eden. This myth has had a profound effect on Judaism and Christianity, but in the East the serpent or dragon has had a positive connotation.

The serpent was feminine in many cultures. The Gnostics honored Eve and the serpent for providing the essential knowledge that made human beings human. The Middle East used to regard the female serpent as the embodiment of enlightenment, or wisdom, because she understood the mysteries of life. In India the serpent was called the mother of all that moves, and named this female serpent Kundalini. She represented the inner power of the human body and the aim is to awaken this Kundalini serpent in the body. (See THE WOMAN'S DICTIONARY by Barbara G. Walker.)

For our writing the Serpent Energy is the feminine aspect of the Godhead which has been so profoundly ignored by Christianity.

I should like to review now the many different cultures which have had the serpent or the snake as a main symbol in their religion and which they worshiped. In each culture the serpent was feminine.

In Africa, Australia and the Amazon they had the Rainbow Serpent which brought rain. In Canaan, Mesopotamia and Africa, Astarte had the sacred serpent wound around her body with the head emerging from the forehead at the Third Eye position. This was a sign that the serpent power had raised from the lower chakra to the sixth chakra symbolizing centeredness in spirit.

In India, Shakti, the serpent energy, is defined as spiritual power that creates and maintains the Universe. It is the coming together of Shakti(feminine moving energy) and Shiva (masculine energy, the unmoving, transcendent divine consciousness) that brings what we call the Mystic Marriage or Enlightenment, called Samadhi by the Hindu.

In Sumer this goddess was called Nina or Nintu and was a serpent-tailed or fish-tailed woman and goddess of writing and life. There were many Sumerian goddesses. Inanna was another goddess, whose symbol was a serpent coiled around a staff. The staff is a symbol of the spine.

In Egypt we are familiar with the serpent at the Third Eye position in deities and royalty. This is called the Uraeus. She, the serpent, was called the Cobra Goddess or Uazit.

When traveling in Mexico, China, in Ireland, in Britain we are not only aware of the serpent carvings but the spiral that is carved in the rocks and religious buildings. The spiral of three and a half turns is like the three and a half turns the Kundalini is coiled at the base of the spine. This secret teaching on the spiral has been known for thousands of years.

Australian primitives had the Rainbow Serpent. It is also in Cuba, Puerto Rico, Brazil, Haitian voodoo, and in Greece. It unites heaven and earth, male and female. (See RAINBOW SERPENT by Robert Garner.) According to the Australian myth, the Rainbow Serpent made the world and gave birth to all people.

Greece had its Gaia as Creator. These images were closely associated with the sacred serpent called Delphyna, Python and Typhon. The god Aesculapius had a serpent entwined around his staff as his symbol of healing.

Ireland, the land of the primitive Celts, had its Brigit, a goddess. The first day of the Celtic spring Birgit breathed life into the mouth of dead winter. She was indicated as a serpent and a symbol of regeneration.

In Mexico the plumed serpent is found at ancient monuments and pyramids. This plumed serpent, called Coatl, is said to symbolize the union of opposites, the synthesis of heaven and earth, a combination of bird and snake. This union of opposites fits our teaching. Quetzalcoatl was the god of the Aztecs. (See THE SERPENT AND

174

THE GODDESS by Mary Condren for additional information on the goddess serpent.)

So what happened in the West to this ancient symbol for regeneration, for fertilization? According to Mary Condren (page 132) the image of the serpent as good, died under the "heel of Mary," the Christian Church. (Mary Condren is writing from an Irish viewpoint.) She explains that the serpent had good and evil qualities from the age of Eve. The age of Brigit saw good and bad serpents. But the age of the Catholic Church crushed the serpent and identified it with the Devil. This Devil was an enemy of Good. God the Father was responsible for all Good. Women were plunged into oppression by the Church. The goddess worship was killed and the Serpent Energy took on an evil hue. She wrote that what she and others are trying to do is to restore this serpent image to a place of Divine Spirituality with all the Goodness that the Father God has been endowed with by the church institution.

Other authors have approached the universality of the serpent image from the viewpoint of its masculine or feminine identity. Rosalyn L. Bruyere in her Volume I of WHEELS OF LIGHT has this to say:

> "I discovered that mythically the serpent has been both masculine and feminine. . . . The phallic image is at once obvious; and, when the serpent is viewed as swallower, the female organ is also implied. . . . The ancient Goddess religion (5700-1500 B.C.), which predates the religion of the male Deity by several thousand years, existed in Egypt and Delphi and Eleusis; she existed throughout a multitude of cultures. . . . In each of these cultures the goddess represented the universal feminine principle of generation and regeneration. . . . Furthermore, the ancient Goddess religion revered the snake above all images, as it was seen to represent the feminine principle and feminine power." (pages 125-126, Edited)

This explanation is important for in our Bible we have had this Divine Energy referred to as masculine. This is a result of the patriarchal worship of the masculine God. This Energy can be used for either, or both, generation and regeneration.

Now why is this important to us of the 1990s?

Why should we go into such detail and be interested in the training and discipline necessary to activate the Kundalini? Why should one care about activating this Divine Energy? I can only speak profoundly from my own experience. Later I shall discuss the conclusions of Gopi Krishna.

I believe that the portals were opened, the gate was cracked, at the beginning of my Search. I had learned about a Hindu, Paramahansa Yogananda, who had come from India to America to bring together the teaching of Jesus Christ and Hinduism. I went to hear a disciple of Yogananda who later gave each student Shaktipat. I knew nothing of being touched by a person whose Kundalini was active, but when he touched my Third Eye the force was so great that I fell back and he caught me. I did not understand then, but now I know that my Kundalini was awakened. After that experience I devoted much time to reading whatever came my way, to studying the AUTOBIOGRAPHY OF A YOGI by Paramahansa Yogananda, and I began to meditate regularly. I also studied psychic phenomena. However, I did not have an opening of my chakras until several years later. This was Grace abounding, for if it had come earlier I might have turned away from my Journey.

I found a book (or it found me) by Gopi Krishna, KUNDALINI, THE EVOLUTIONARY ENERGY IN MAN. This assured me that I had nothing to fear as long as I was centered in the Spirit. Reading it caused a movement of the Energy and I began to experience Bliss.

I was led to have dream interpretation by a Jungian analyst who understood the Kundalini movement. The dreams were conducive to my accepting the opening of the chakras by the flowing of this Divine Energy. I had many experiences of the circulating of the Energy and I can only explain the results by inadequate words such as Ecstasy, Bliss, Love, Fullness, Joy, Glory and deep Gratitude. (I should add that I was living a celibate life.) Through this time I was being prepared for my writing and the Energy was flowing freely. In meditation during the Christmas Season of 1978 I was given my Commission to write an interpretation of the Book of Revelation. This was a true miracle as I had never read the Book of Revelation; indeed, I had never studied the Bible to any extent.

As I began writing REVELATION: FOR A NEW AGE, I began feeling the Kundalini moving more and more. Much of that book was written from my intuitive Knowing and my intellect expanded as I listened to my Inner Voice and wrote what came to my intellect. The Holy Spirit, the Kundalini, is the Inner Voice.

Through the years I have had serious physical illnesses which relate to the opening of the chakras. At one time, when seriously ill, I had a Near Death Experience which I understand now was another opening by the Kundalini. I was well grounded in the Spirit and came through these illnesses with a deeper awareness of the Spirit and lost all fear of death.

I have described these experiences in the hope that they will resonate with some experience the reader has had. Much of our Christian literature has not given us the answers to the questions raised by these experiences. Now, of course there are Westerners who are writing about this Inner Spring of Joy and are teaching others through various types of Yoga how to activate it.

A note of caution must enter in here. This is the Energy of the Universe we are speaking about. It is not to be played with. It takes deep devotion to the spiritual Path to make it a safe choice for our own spiritual advancement. One who misuses it for selfish physical or emotional highs will have a negative reaction—a reaction that may devastate their physical and emotional health. The "high" reached through use of drugs of various kinds can also be devastating as they become habit-forming and interfere with, indeed block, the elevation of spiritual consciousness.

Gopi Krishna writes extensively in his book KUNDALINI; THE EVOLUTIONARY ENERGY IN MAN about the negative effects. They came on him and he was ignorant of the cause or how to rid himself of the burning pain, the hallucinations, the physical harm to his body. He warns about the misuse of this energy but gives some suggestions as to how to balance it to get rid of negative results. The positive results are beyond description. He taught that the activating of this Energy from the base chakra to the head area would bring one to a high intellectual level—a genius level. His main theme in later years was to encourage more scientific investigation of it.

This is a very limited background for my Thesis but I believe that we should become aware of this great potential for our advanced Spiritual Knowing. I encourage others to study this Energy in their own experience. As Christians we need to become aware of its potential to raise us to a higher consciousness. The Christian mystics have written about it in rather abstract language, but it is there. We are God-Beings with this power within which will lift us to realization of our Oneness with that Universal Energy.

Because of my belief, I have studied the Holy Bible deeply for clues to this teaching hidden therein. With the substantial foundation from the teachings of Moses, the Prophets, Jesus Christ and St.

Paul, you may have the desire to build your own belief about the Kundalini energy.

Through meditation, prayer, reading spiritual books, study of Eastern religions, practice of yoga, massage and other alternative energy treatments, this Energy can be aroused. Know your Blessing and go forth in Oneness with that Divinity we call God. Your Inner Spirit is your Guide!

Your Thousand-Petaled Lotus will shine!!

BIBLIOGRAPHY

Bailey, Alice. FROM BETHLEHEM TO CALVARY, New York, NY: Lucis Publishing, 1981.

Bruyere, Rosalyn L. Edited by Jeanne Farrens, WHEELS OF LIGHT A STUDY OF THE CHAKRAS, Volume 1, Sierra Madre, CA: Bon Productions, 1991.

Bucke, Richard Maurice, M.D. COSMIC CONSCIOUSNESS. New York, NY: E. P. Dutton, 1969.

Churchward, James. THE COSMIC FORCES OF MU, New York, NY: Coronet Communications, 1972.

Cirlót, J.E. A DICTIONARY OF SYMBOLS, New York, NY: Philosophical Library, 1981.

Condren, Mary. THE SERPENT AND THE GODDESS, San Francisco, CA: Harper and Row, 1989.

Cooper, David. SILENCE, SIMPLICITY, AND SOLITUDE, New York, NY: Crown Publishing, 1992.

CRUDEN'S COMPLETE CONCORDANCE, Grand Rapids, MI: Zondervan Publishing, 1982.

Davis, Roy E. GOD HAS GIVEN US EVERY GOOD THING, Lakemont, GA: CSA Press, 1986.

Edinger, Edward F. THE BIBLE AND THE PSYCHE, Toronto, CAN: Inner City Books, 1986.

Elder, Dorothy. REVELATION FOR A NEW AGE (THE BOOK OF REVELATION), Marina del Rey, CA: DeVorss & Co., 1988.

———— WOMEN OF THE BIBLE SPEAK TO WOMEN OF TODAY, Marina del Rey, CA: DeVorss & Co., 1986.

———— FROM METAPHYSICAL TO MYSTICAL, Denver, CO: Doriel Publishing, 1994.

———— THE SONG OF SONGS AND ENLIGHTENMENT. Marina del Rey, CA: DeVorss & Co., 1988.

Fillmore, Charles. ATOM SMASHING POWER OF MIND, Unity Village, MO: Unity School of Christianity, 1949.

————— TWELVE POWERS OF MAN, Unity Village, MO: Unity School of Christianity, 1934

————— METAPHISICAL BIBLE DICTIONARY, Unity Village, MO: Unity School of Christianity, 1931.

————— REVEALING WORD, Unity Village, MO: Unity School of Christianity, 1931.

Fox, Matthew. BREAKTHROUGH: MEISTER ECKHART'S CREATION SPIRITUALITY IN NEW TRANSLATION, New York, NY: Doubleday, 1980.

————— ILLUMINATIONS OF HILDEGARD OF BINGEN, Santa Fe, NM: Bear & Company, 1985.

————— THE COMING OF THE COSMIC CHRIST, San Francisco, CA: Harper & Row, 1988.

Garner, Robert L. THE RAINBOW SERPENT, Toronto, CAN: Inner City Books, 1990.

Goldsmith, Joel. THE MYSTICAL I, New York, NY: Harper & Row, 1971.

Heline, Corinne. NEW AGE BIBLE INTERPRETATION Vol. I–VI, Los Angeles, CA: New Age Press, 1935-54.

Halifax, Joan. SHAMAN, THE WOUNDED HEALER, New York, NY: Thames & Hudson, 1982.

Hixon, Lex. COMING HOME, New York, NY: Jeremy P. Tarcher, Inc., 1989.

Hoffman, Edward. THE WAY OF SPLENDOR, Northvale, New Jersey: Jason Aronson Inc., 1989.

Hopkins, Emma Curtis. BIBLE INTERPRETATIONS SERIES 1, Marina del Rey, CA: DeVorss & Co.

————— HIGH MYSTICISM, Marina del Rey, CA: DeVorss & Co., 1974.

————— SCIENTIFIC CHRISTIAN MENTAL PRACTICE, Marina del Rey, CA: DeVorss & Co.

Hubbard, Barbara Marx. THE REVELATION: OUR CRISIS IN BIRTH, Sonoma, CA: Foundation for Conscious Evolution, 1993.

Johnson, Elizabeth A. SHE WHO IS, New York, NY: Crossroad Publishing, 1992.

Joy, Brugh, M.D. JOY'S WAY, New York, NY: J.P. Tarcher, Inc., 1979.

Jung, Carl. SYMBOLS OF TRANSFORMATION, Princeton, NJ: Princeton University Press, Bollinger Series XX, 1976.

————— AION, Princeton, NJ: Princeton University Press, Bollingen Series XX, 1978.

Keating, Thomas. OPEN MIND, OPEN HEART, Rockport, MA: Element, Inc., 1986.

———— THE MYSTERY OF CHRIST, Warwick, NY: Amity House, 1987.

King, Serge. KAHUNA HEALING, Wheaton, IL: Theosophical Publishing House, 1983.

Krishna, Gopi. KUNDALINI, THE EVOLUTIONARY ENERGY IN MAN, Boston, MA: Shambala, 1970.

———— KUNDALINI FOR THE NEW AGE, Edited by Gene Kieffer, New York, NY: Bantam Books, 1988.

Leadbeater, C.W. THE CHAKRAS, Wheaton, IL: Theosophical Publishing House, 1972.

Long, Max Freedom. THE HUNA CODE IN RELIGIONS, Marina del Rey, CA: DeVorss & Co., 1987.

Muktananda, Swami. WHERE ARE YOU GOING, South Fallsberg, NY: SYDA Foundation, 1989.

Myss, Caroline, Ph.D. ANATOMY OF THE SPIRIT, New York, Harmony Books, 1996.

NAG HAMMADI LIBRARY, James M. Robinson, Gen. Ed., San Francisco, CA: Harper & Row, 1981.

Pagels, Elaine. THE GNOSTIC GOSPELS, New York, NY: Vintage Books, 1981.

Paramahansa Yogananda. AUTOBIOGRAPHY OF A YOGI, Los Angeles, CA: Self Realization Fellowship, 1969.

———— THE SECOND COMING OF CHRIST, Dallas, TX: Amrita Foundation, Inc., 1982.

Sanford, John. HEALING AND WHOLENESS, New York, NY: Paulist Press, 1977.

Sannella, Lee, M.D. THE KUNDALINI EXPERIENCE, Lower Lake, CA: Integral Publishing, 1992.

Shah, Idries. THE SUFIS, Garden City, NY: Doubleday & Co., Anchor Books, 1971.

Singer, June. BOUNDARIES OF THE SOUL, THE PRACTICE OF JUNG'S PSYCHOLOGY, Garden City, NJ: Anchor Books, 1972.

Skarin, Annalee, YE ARE GODS, New York, NY: Philosophical Library, 1952.

Spong, John Shelby. RESCUING THE BIBLE FROM FUNDAMENTALISM, San Francisco, CA: Harper/Collins, 1991.

St. John of the Cross, LIVING FLAME OF LOVE, Mahwah, NJ: Newman Press, 1962.

Stone, Merlin. WHEN GOD WAS A WOMAN, New York, NY: Harcourt Brace Jovanovich, 1976.

Teilhard de Chardin, Pierre. THE PHENOMENON OF MAN, New York, NY: Harper & Row, 1965.

Troward, Thomas. BIBLE MYSTERY AND BIBLE MEANING, New York, NY: Dodd, Mead & Co., 1913.

———— THE DORE LECTURES, New York, NY: Dodd, Mead & Co., 1909.

Underhill, Evelyn. MYSTICISM, Cleveland, OH: World Publishing Co., 1967.

Walker, Barbara G. THE WOMAN'S DICTIONARY, San Francisco, CA: Harper Collins, 1988.

Wilhelm, Richard, Translator. SECRET OF THE GOLDEN FLOWER, New York, NY: Harcourt, Brace & World, Inc., 1962.

WORLD SCRIPTURE, A COMPARATIVE ANTHOLOGY OF SACRED TEXTS, International Religious Foundation, New York, NY: Paragon House, 1991.

GLOSSARY

AIN SOPH: Incomprehensible state of pure Being (Cabala); Boundless Being

ANDROGYNY: A state of perfect balance between the masculine and feminine elements in the psyche; Oneness; Wholeness.

ANIMA: The feminine in the psyche of a man.

ANIMUS: The masculine in the psyche of a woman.

ATMA: Soul; Divine Self.

BUDDHI: Higher Intelligence.

COLLECTIVE UNCONSCIOUS: The totality of beliefs, thoughts, memories, feelings and experiences of the human race.

GENERATION: Procreation; reproduction.

GODHEAD: The Essence of the Creator; Pure Consciousness.

LIBIDO: Divine Creative force of nature (Jung); sexual energy (Freud).

MANDALA: A universal symbol of Wholeness; a depiction of the center of the mind of God; a focus for meditation conducive to mystic exaltation.

RACE CONSCIOUSNESS: The beliefs, actions, mores of that society in which we live that affects our choices.

REGENERATION: Changing the body from the physical to the spiritual; spiritual body is called celestial body (Paul); uniting body, mind, spirit into Oneness.

SATORI: A Zen term for Enlightenment.

SELF: (Capital S) Inner Divine Presence of the soul; the Christ.

SELF: (small s) ego, personality (self).

SERPENT FIRE: Kundalini.

SHADOW: A Jungian term. That whixh is in the unconscious which is a dark side of our personality. It is often a characteristic projected onto others; it covers the Soul consciousness.

SHAKTI: The Divine Cosmic Power; Chi; Kundalini; Serpent Energy.

SHAKTIPAT: The transmission of spiritual power (Shakti) from the Guru to the disciple; spiritual awakening by grace.

SHIVA: All pervasive Supreme Reality; the consort of Shakti.

SUSHUMNA: The central channel of the subtle body, located in the spine.

TEMENOS: A term used by Jung to designate a place apart from the world, a sacred place.

BIOGRAPHICAL SKETCH

Dorothy Elder has been a student of world religions, the metaphysical and mystical path of many Seekers, and has combined Christian teachings and those world religions in many of her books. The teachings of Carl Jung, her own personal experience with the Inner Divine Energy and her creativity, makes this book almost an account of a personal spiritual Journey. She has experienced marriage and children, a career as a counselor in public education, and an inspired writer of twelve books. Her Purpose is to share spiritual insighs with those who are led to seeking a mystical Path. An esoteric interpretation of Scripture is her way of bringing forth a spiritual meaning. A book on the Old Testament and the Kundalini will be published at a future date.

OTHER BOOKS
BY DOROTHY ELDER

REVELATION: FOR A NEW AGE
(The Book of Revelation)

WOMEN OF THE BIBLE SPEAK TO WOMEN OF TODAY

THE SONG OF SONGS AND ENLIGHTENMENT

FROM METAPHYSICAL TO MYSTICAL

PROOF OF THE TRUTH
(A Biography of Dr. Grace Faus)

HEAVEN IS HERE
(A Collection of Poetry)